"I have rarely had as visceral a reaction to a book as I had in reading Maya Smart's brilliant and life-changing *Reading for Our Lives*. Like her namesake Maya Angelou, who suffered childhood trauma and couldn't speak, only to become a world-class orator and writer, Maya Smart helps us to navigate the perilous but fulfilling route from birth to literacy in the first six years of life. This is a book that every parent must read to make sure their children reach their full potential as readers and citizens of our nation."

—**Michael Eric Dyson,** coauthor of
Represent: The Unfinished Fight for the Vote

"A *must-read* for any parent! This exceptional book walks you through not only the *why* of reading to your child but the *way*. The scientifically grounded, step-by-step insights outlined here can heighten both your and your child's joy at learning one of life's most important skills: reading."

—**Barbara Oakley,** author of *A Mind for Numbers*

"I anticipate a revolution of reading readiness once parents get their hands on this book! Preparing children at home so that they are equipped for school is a gift any parent can easily give with Smart's book in hand. I'll be recommending *Reading for Our Lives* for years to come. It's the best book about learning to read I've ever read!"

—**Julie Bogart,** creator and founder of Brave Writer, author of
The Brave Learner and *Raising Critical Thinkers*

"An amazing book for perhaps the most important job parents have: getting our kids to love to read."

—**Ryan Holiday,** #1 *New York Times* bestselling author of *The Daily Stoic, The Obstacle Is the Way,* and *Ego Is the Enemy*

"This book is a wonderful resource for families with young children as it recognizes them as the child's 'first teachers.' It weaves together an introduction to early literacy through the child's ages and stages with recommendations that support raising a reader!"

—**Ann McClain Terrell,** early-childhood education consultant and National Association for the Education of Young Children past president

"*Reading for Our Lives* is the book to turn to when nurturing critical readers. Like reading, Smart's book is for our children's lives. Don't miss out, because our kids must not miss out on the life-giving power of reading."

—**Ibram X. Kendi,** National Book Award–winning author of *Stamped from the Beginning* and *How to Be an Antiracist*

READING FOR OUR LIVES

*The Urgency of Early Literacy and the
Action Plan to Help Your Child*

Maya Payne Smart

AVERY
an imprint of Penguin Random House
New York

AVERY

an imprint of Penguin Random House LLC
1745 Broadway, New York, NY 10019
penguinrandomhouse.com

Most Avery books are available at special quantity discounts for bulk purchase for sales promotions, premiums, fund-raising, and educational needs. Special books or book excerpts also can be created to fit specific needs. For details, write SpecialMarkets@penguinrandomhouse.com.

The Library of Congress has catalogued the hardcover edition as follows:

Names: Smart, Maya Payne, author.
Title: Reading for our lives: a literacy action plan from birth to six / Maya Payne Smart.
Description: New York: Avery, Penguin Random House LLC, 2022. | Includes index.
Identifiers: LCCN 2022010712 (print) | LCCN 2022010713 (ebook) | ISBN 9780593332177 (hardcover) | ISBN 9780593332184 (epub)
Subjects: LCSH: Reading (Elementary) | Children—Books and reading. | Readiness for school.
Classification: LCC LB1573.S67 2022 (print) | LCC LB1573 (ebook) | DDC 372.4—dc23/eng/20220425
LC record available at https://lccn.loc.gov/2022010712 LC ebook record available at https://lccn.loc.gov/2022010713

Trade paperback ISBN 9780593544426

Previously published as *Reading for Our Lives: A Literacy Action Plan from Birth to Six*

Excerpt from the poem "Book Power" by Gwendolyn Brooks on page 27 reprinted by Consent of Brooks Permissions.

Printed in the United States of America
1st Printing

The authorized representative in the EU for product safety and compliance is Penguin Random House Ireland, Morrison Chambers, 32 Nassau Street, Dublin D02 YH68, Ireland. https://eu-contact.penguin.ie.

For Zora, my daughter and inspiration.
Without you, this book would surely not exist.

CONTENTS

We Should All Be Readers

The question is not whether we can afford to invest in every child; it is whether we can afford not to.

—Marian Wright Edelman

The Quiet Crisis

Heavy rain once filled our local water supply with so much silt and debris that treatment systems failed. For the next seven days, local authorities and media raised the alarm that residents should boil their water or risk illness. Restaurants shut down. Families bought bottled water by the shelf-full. Hospitals procured truckloads of certified water and switched operating rooms to alternative sterilization methods. Once the boil notice was lifted, we all flushed our pipes, dumped ice machines, and resumed life and work as usual.

The crisis was obvious and urgent. The response clear and immediate. The end apparent.

What's happening with our nation's pipeline to reading, if

you can call it that, is just as urgent, yet hidden. There is no infrastructure in place to raise a nation of readers, let alone a coordinated response to breakdowns.

We lack the basic systems of care, communication, connection, and family support required to nurture critical language and literacy skills in children from birth. We focus time, attention, and resources on the school years, neglecting the foundational brain, language, and social development upon which school and life success rest.

Our results speak for themselves. Basic literacy skills among U.S. adults are weak overall (despite relatively high levels of education) and low literacy is unusually persistent across generations, judged by international standards. About one in six U.S. adults has low literacy skills, compared to, for example, one in twenty in Japan. That's approximately 36 million U.S. adults (roughly equal to the combined populations of New York, Michigan, and Minnesota) who can't compare and contrast written information, make low-level inferences, or locate information within a multipart document. And worse still, socially disadvantaged parents in the U.S., compared to those in other countries, are more likely to pass on weaker skills to their children.

Completing medical forms, reading prescription instructions, parsing a voting ballot, and grasping employment or housing contract details are all challenging, if not impossible, tasks for far too many. The huge disconnect between the reading skills many Americans have and those they *need* affects their health, wellness, employment, housing, and even likelihood of incarceration.

But here's the part that all parents must understand: this crisis brews early. The tragedy of low adult literacy has its roots in infancy, when everyday early experiences launch lifelong learning trajectories.

Children's brains form more than a million new neural connections per second during the first few years of life, and future brain development rests on the soundness or fragility of those earliest links. In fact, evidence from anatomical, physiological, and gene-expression studies all suggest that basic brain architecture is in place by around 2 years old, and later brain development is mostly about "refining the major circuits and networks that are already established." And critically, it's caregivers' nurturing, supportive back-and-forth verbal engagement in a child's first years that literally stimulates brain function and shapes brain structure.

If the tilt of a child's learning trajectory is too low or flat at the start, it's hard to reach expected levels of literacy during the school years and nearly impossible after. A slow start hurts a child's prospects much more than dropping out of school early. When a child enters school without the language skills, alphabetic knowledge, and social development to take advantage of grade-level instruction, it requires extraordinary acts of parent advocacy to navigate the phalanx of teachers, administrators, specialists, and paperwork required to get that child proper support to play catch-up.

For most children, the worst-case scenario isn't complete illiteracy—and for this reason, the issue can remain off the radar of caring parents who assume that their children will eventually learn to read. Rather, the greater threat for many is the pain of an unnecessarily hard climb to barely proficient reading. It's the frustration, demoralization, and low self-esteem that comes from struggling mightily to learn how letters and sounds connect. It's the grueling labor of rigidly, robotically sounding out words without the fluency or automaticity to grasp their meaning individually, let alone within whole sentences, paragraphs, passages, or pages. It's the heartbreak of poor performance in math and other subjects when the nuances of course content, assignment details, and test instructions are missed. It's the disappointment and stagnation of reading capacity that never quite measures up to the demands of the college, the job, or the life they dream of.

Doing time in school—for years—without ever receiving effective reading instruction is a special kind of torture that adds student shame to educational sham. For too long, as a nation we've tested school-aged kids, reported the results, and acted like oversight is a reading achievement delivery system. But literacy doesn't flow from federal mandates through state assessments and district policy to classroom instruction and students' brains. Standardized assessments are valuable, but limited, *alert* systems. Mere indicators, they can sound when our educational system fails to meet certain expectations. But they don't illuminate the root causes of that failure or tell us what to do about them. Alarms ring; they don't teach. And often when an alarm rings for too long, we tune it out.

Today, alarms abound. In the U.S., 5-year-olds have "significantly lower" emergent literacy than kids in other countries that have comprehensive early-childhood education and national paid parental leave. Just one-third of a nationally representative sample of U.S. fourth- and eighth-grade students scored at a proficient level in the latest National Assessment of Educational Progress. Reading scores of the lowest-performing 9- and 13-year-olds have dropped since 2012, reaching lows in reading levels that we haven't witnessed since the 1970s. And—most devastatingly—just 14 percent of U.S. 15-year-olds read well enough to comprehend lengthy texts, handle abstract or counterintuitive concepts, and evaluate content and information sources to separate fact from opinion.

And don't get me started on the state of children's reading interest and enjoyment. National surveys reveal skyrocketing percentages of 13-year-olds who say they "never or hardly ever" read for fun—31 percent in a recent survey, compared with 8 percent in 1984.

The sad truth is this: for the past few decades, the majority of American kids have been shuffled from grade to grade without ever reading well enough. And we're not talking about children with profound learning or intellectual disabilities. These are capable students whose reading development is hobbled by a devastating mix of untapped opportunity at home and inadequate instruction in schools.

Incredibly, that's despite the fact that elementary schools devote more time to English, reading, and language arts than anything else—often more than 30 percent of designated "instructional time." In reality, much of that time is misspent on activities that don't directly teach what kids need to know about how written language works. Teachers struggle to meet the diverse needs of learners who arrive in their classrooms with little knowledge of the alphabet, the sounds of English, and the relationships between letters and sounds. They have trouble instilling these basics of the alphabetic code, let alone developing kids' oral language, vocabulary, and background knowledge so they can comprehend words in print.

We can't afford to continue pretending that a hodgepodge of reactivity and remediation can get millions of children reading well enough to flourish. We can't leave whole populations without the skills, knowledge, and community support that underpin full participation in society and expect things to turn out well for them or for us. We all suffer when we don't muster the collective will, skill, and integrity to ensure that every child learns to read.

To attain the consciousness, solidarity, and equity our society so desperately needs, we must be informed and deliberate in nourishing early literacy. So, too, if we are to engender the level of citizenship, critical thinking, and limitless potential that our children and society deserve. And because the odds of success are set before school begins, we've got to start at home.

Parents and early caregivers hold the key. Period. We will never see the promise of mass literacy fulfilled until parents— our children's first teachers—understand how reading skills develop and how to spur them along.

The Missing Manual

Parents know that our children need to be strong readers to navigate school and life, and we want to help them thrive. We know that we have a role to play, whether it's reading aloud to our kids, teaching them the alphabet, or helping them sound out words. But we tend to be fuzzy on the specifics and aren't sure that we have the knowledge to impart the right skills, the right way, at the right time. We worry that what we're doing now might not adequately prepare our children for what they'll need later. We crave validation that we and they are on track. Or worse, we assume that we don't need to think about academics just yet, only to be caught unprepared when kids struggle later.

Early concern about reading is justified, especially given the heightened demands of today's global society and postindustrial economy. We've experienced for ourselves the crucible of continuous learning, training, and development to garner new skills and master new technology amid constant change and new complexities. We know that growth-oriented, high-paying jobs are less and less attainable for poor readers. Clearly, the labor market rewards readers when increasing levels of literacy are required just to navigate the job listings, qualifications, and applications to find and win employment.

Parents frequently tell me they feel stretched too thin by the growing and competing demands of work, education, and family. They struggle to consistently find the time or energy to help their children move toward reading and writing (or later, reading and writing *better*). They say things like:

> *"I have a little bit of shame around this, but I have not been the best about reading to my daughter. I try and she just pushes the book away."*
>
> *"There's so much conflicting advice out there. I have no idea what's best. I constantly question myself, wondering, 'Am I doing this right?'"*

"One of our biggest guilt things that nags us as parents is that the kids don't get individual time to work on the things they need to work on. With three kids, it's just overwhelming."

Do any of these statements sound familiar? If so, this book is for you. I wrote it for parents who know that reading skills matter and who want to play a thoughtful, active, and effective role in nurturing them. I'll show you how to build literacy through everyday activities and how to advocate for high-quality instruction when your child goes to school. With this book in hand, your raise-a-reader education has begun.

My Journey

On the night my dad died, I walked to his bedside to show him a black-and-white sonogram, glossy and blurred. It may have been the first time I ever approached him while he was lying down. In my memories, he was always up—reading the newspaper at the kitchen table, mowing the lawn or shoveling snow, laboring over files in his office, watching some dark TV drama. I remember the picture feeling light and flimsy in the enormity of the moment, a father on his deathbed hearing his only child tell of the life she carried.

He took in the sound waves rendered in print, smiled, and whispered, *I think it's a boy, but I hope it's a girl.* He got his wish, but I never got to ask him what he meant by it. He passed within hours of his quiet declaration and left me to puzzle over the spaces between a parent's dreams and a child's promise, between presence and absence, between birth and legacy.

When our baby girl was born months later, my husband and I named her after Zora Neale Hurston to foretell a wise, bold, and colorful life. Like my parents did when they named me after Maya Angelou, we set the intention of resilience, fortitude, and distinction upon her young shoulders. We vowed to help our Zora experience the fullness of her inheritance—to discover herself as powerful, unique, and inseparable from all the life that pulses everywhere. Or, as her namesake put it, to know that each of us is "the world and the heavens boiled down to a drop."

I made reading—the miracle of connecting with others across space and time—a pillar of my mothering. In our first days at home, the intimacy of sharing stories and books became a touchstone. I recited lines from Jabari Asim's *Girl of Mine* from dawn till dusk. *Giggly, wiggly precious pearl. I'm so glad that you're my girl.* That little board book held my dreams for my daughter, held my awe of her existence. Reading it over and over felt like love and life support for a sleep-deprived mom. Soon I'd memorized the text, turning the pages only for show as I kept on rocking, reading, feeding her.

As a new mom who'd just lost a parent, I was comforted by the story's easy rhythms and my own belief in the power of a parent's words in a child's ear. Knowing firsthand how words nourish, I wanted to feed her page upon page, give her tastes of poetry, let her sip prose. I felt the book's upbeat refrain bolster something precious and fragile in her—and in me. Reading to her was love, care, and a pathway to a family ethos that I treasured. Toni

Morrison said, "We die. That may be the meaning of life. But we do language. That may be the measure of our lives."

Stories were our first, most cherished language. I threw myself into the quest to raise a reader with all the zeal of new motherhood and the passion of someone who has lived the written word's power to both uplift and inspire. Soon, though, I was ready to expand my repertoire of literacy-promoting activities. But what to add? The advice in the books on my shelf, and in the articles I consumed voraciously, seemed to start and stop with storytime.

I put Zora in a Montessori toddler program for some professional backup. There, she gained other valuable skills through baby-doll washing and moving pompoms from one dish to another with tongs. Her fine motor skills, potty training, and home-tidying abilities blossomed, but I remained unsure about her reading development. Were the verbal experiences, social interactions, and classroom read-alouds enough? Was I doing my part at home?

The knowledge that parents need about reading development and instruction is not easy to come by. The United States invests little in children in their first few years of life, when the brain is at its most flexible to build a foundation for learning, social engagement, and health. There's no mass early-literacy boot camp for parents; valuable research is locked behind paywalls and inaccessible to the public; and too few experts communicate their findings in clear, understandable, and practical terms. Most librarians and booksellers are pros at helping you locate what they've stocked, but less adept at explaining how to facilitate language and literacy learning at different ages and stages.

I remember wandering the aisles of bookstores selecting the "best," most beautiful picture books for my newborn. I knew she couldn't lift her head or even see well yet. But I didn't know that a photo of a human face or a bold pattern would catch her attention more than the lush illustrations of a Caldecott Medal winner. And while I knew to talk to my baby, I didn't get that it was a two-way street from day one, that her coos and babbles were as significant as the words I spoke.

In short, I made every mistake in the book—if there had been such a book. Oh, how I wished there were a book (maybe with a title like *What to Deliver After You've Delivered*), preferably with a job description, manual of procedures, and performance metrics. But like so much of parenting, no clear instructions came with the position.

So I went back to school myself, enrolling in a graduate course at the Curry School of Education at the University of Virginia to get the literacy lowdown. I learned that there was more—much more—that I could do to unlock long-term reading and educational success for Zora. I also discovered that what I'd thought was personal ignorance (*I* didn't know how to teach reading) was actually a national crisis. Parents were far from the only ones missing a clear sense of how reading skills develop and the knowledge needed to nurture them. Teachers, pediatricians, and educational policymakers often lacked this critical insight as well. Most classmates in the Foundations of Reading Instruction course were teachers, and while they knew more than me, they had much to learn, too.

I quickly discovered that being a strong reader scarcely prepares you to teach reading. In fact, many fluent readers aren't consciously aware of the underlying structure of language and print that good teaching must make explicit for children. In order to help kids, parents—and certainly teachers—need to learn to attend to and describe features of written language that expert readers no longer notice or focus on.

The contrast between (on one hand) abysmal reading performance and (on the other) superficial advice doled out to parents about how to raise readers rankled. Surely the parents who shape a child's reading prospects *for years* before the child enters school should be better informed.

Without any mom-in-the-trenches guidance, I set out to document what I learned about how reading works, how parents can foster it, and what we can (and can't) expect from instruction in schools. I scoured academic literature, reading curricula, state learning standards, government reports, and more. I talked to teachers, tutors, and parents in the thick of raising readers. I served on school, library, and literacy nonprofit boards; volunteered in early-learning programs; and developed databases of research and instructional techniques. I also called top researchers to ask what specific advice they would offer parents today.

My personal effort to better understand what it takes to raise a reader tipped into a larger mission to help all parents learn what's needed to do this vital work.

Why You Need an Action Plan for Your Family

For this book, I've traced the path to literacy from birth through early elementary school with stories and science that illuminate the ways we can influence our kids' success. I hope to give you clear guidance on what to do, when, how, and why.

You may be thinking that plenty of parents set their kids up for educational and career success without a plan. That they bought some picture books, read to kids regularly, enrolled them in good schools, and voilà! But the fact is, a more expansive approach is both possible and invaluable today because of the increasing demands of modern work, school, and life. Your aim isn't to do what proved sufficient for some in previous generations, but rather to do what's likely to prepare your child to reach their full potential.

We'd be foolish to take a back seat, given the indisputable evidence of our power to launch a child's literacy. Research shows, for example, that the number of turn-taking interactions toddlers had in conversations with adults predicted their IQ and language skills *ten years later* as middle schoolers. For most of us, the optimal level of talk requires serious intention, backed by well-designed habits, especially given today's busier lifestyles.

And let's be honest, parents across the income and privilege spectrums need reminders to fully engage with kids' language and literacy development. With increasing demands on our time and growing distractions, such as our ever-alluring smartphones and diminishing work-family boundaries, we have the potential to be less purposeful and responsive than we might otherwise.

What parents can accomplish easily early on, through nurturing and natural conversation, may require hard, time-consuming, expensive remediation to catch up on later. Kids need a base level of language proficiency entering kindergarten to fully benefit from classroom instruction. Kindergarten language skills are the single best predictor of school achievement across all subjects in third and fifth grade. And longitudinal research has found evidence that kids who don't read proficiently by third grade are four times as likely to drop out of school.

Studies of the effectiveness of federally funded programs aimed at improving reading skills in adolescents show that they usually had no effect on reading achievement and sometimes even produced negative ones. Even with interventions that appear to be effective, it's hard to determine the size of gains, and it's unclear if any "statistically significant" improvements that resulted are of *practical* significance—that is, strong enough to boost school performance, job prospects, and overall health and well-being. There's a big difference between a program being better than nothing and being good enough for our kids. And programs with negative outcomes are worse than nothing.

Every child deserves full literacy to thrive, and instilling the strongest possible base prior to school gives a child a real shot at gaining the skills and knowledge they'll need long term. Only time can reveal the costs of being unable to rise to the ever-higher levels of reading and writing required to navigate our global, tech-driven society.

When I was growing up, my dad always told me to front-load my effort. He said, "Work as hard as you can to learn as much as you can as fast as you can." That way, when inevitable distractions and unforeseen circumstances arrived, I'd have some wiggle room. Starting strong creates a chance at recovering from setbacks. So it goes with your child's literacy: you will never find a better time than now to launch a reader.

What You'll Get in This Book

The road to reading is long and winding. From diving into the research, talking to parents about their pain points and frustrations, and raising my own reader, I've learned what parents need: a map, some fuel, a maintenance plan, mile markers, and occasional roadside assistance. You wouldn't embark on any other trip of a lifetime without preparing, would you?

Road Map

Parents need a big-picture understanding of what reading is, its prerequisite and constituent skills, and what to focus on at each age and stage in their child's development. Without a 10,000-foot view of how reading unfolds from infancy to early elementary school, parents can get stuck spinning their wheels on activities that don't meaningfully support their children.

This book maps the early-learning landscape—the skills, resources, and partners we all need. I'll walk you through the critical early-literacy skills and illustrate how they develop: when you should start cultivating them, what mastery looks like, and which milestones lie in between. Plus, you'll gain the perspective to understand how your work as a parent intersects with that of numerous other players, from pediatricians and librarians to teachers and tutors.

Premium Fuel

Parents are often said to be kids' first and best teachers. The "first" part is guaranteed, but the "best" part must be earned. When it comes to literacy, evidence (not intuition) is the best way to judge what works. So this book offers premium fuel in the form of high-quality research findings to power your little one's journey.

Literacy is one of the most studied topics in academia. There were already more than 100,000 studies on how children learn to read in 1999 when Congress convened the National Reading Panel, and the number has continued to climb. Conferences, publications, and whole careers are devoted to bridging the divide between what research in linguistics, psychology, cognitive science, and education tells us about reading development and how we can actually spark and accelerate those developments in children.

This book presents good research in a digestible format so you can use it to inform your decisions and behavior. We all benefit from enhancing our individual experience and perspective with the wisdom of evidence and analysis. Recent discoveries in neuroscience, molecular biology, and epigenetics alongside years of insights from behavioral and social sciences can also boost our empathy by giving us deeper understanding of children's experiences. All this helps us navigate the road to literacy for children more smoothly and efficiently.

Routine Maintenance

Becoming literate involves considerable work for a child's growing brain, but nurturing reading doesn't have to. Beginning in infancy, parents can foster literacy with warmth, responsiveness, dialogue, and turn-taking. Over time these practices can become core habits and make a lasting impact. In this book, I'll provide simple everyday strategies to help you find the perspective and build the muscle needed to relate to your child with intention, consistency, and generosity over the long haul.

The fact is, once parents know what the research says about what kids need (and when), there's the practical matter of doing those things day in and day out . . . for years. For that, we need parent-tested and -approved techniques that are easy to fit into busy lives. Putting the time and energy into establishing strong practices early on can yield lifelong benefits and prevent costly breakdowns.

Mile Markers

While details of every child's reading journey may vary, certain skills and knowledge are typical or desirable at specific ages and stages. This book shares a chronology of language and literacy milestones and targets, so you know what's up ahead and what to watch for.

The goal is foresight and anticipation, not worry or guilt, so think of each "mile marker" as a reminder of the incredible cognitive, motor, language, and literacy growth that's unfolding for your little one. Knowing the specific skills that all kids must gain in time makes you a much savvier teacher—and educational advocate—for your little one.

Roadside Assistance

A lot of parenting media treats families as islands. *Read this and teach that*, the books advise, *and your child will learn, grow, thrive*. But in reality, reading develops within a dynamic web of relationships and experiences. While it's a mistake to rely on schools alone, parents need ongoing support from community members, including friends, family, neighbors, teachers, librarians, and others, to keep their kids on track.

There's often also a role for the just-in-time intervention of specialists, from speech and hearing therapists to learning and reading experts, depending on a child's particular needs. This is the roadside assistance that can be absolutely crucial to reaching your destination—a child who reads and writes to their full potential.

In his book *Raising Kids Who Read*, cognitive scientist Daniel Willingham warns parents to "resist the urge to engage in reading instruction unless you have reason to believe you know what you're doing." He's got a point. I'm calling on all parents to accept the challenge to *learn* what you're doing and *teach* what you can. Your child's education just might depend on it.

Are you ready to get started? The following pages provide a family reading road map, evidence-based fuel for your journey, a routine maintenance manual, mile markers to chart your progress, and tips on finding roadside support for when you feel adrift or need a jump start. Let's go!

1

Beyond Bedtime Stories: The Truth About Getting Kids Ready to Read

Keep in mind always the present you are constructing. It should be the future you want.

—Alice Walker

A mom friend and I had been having a forgettable chat in a picturesque little café when I brought it up—a subject that made her visibly tense.

I'd known her as an unflappable, high-powered management consultant turned tech executive. She was a visionary, always spoiling for a challenge worthy of her considerable skills and talents. Thoughtful and strategic, she brought a commanding yet optimistic presence to meetings and made people want to rise to the heights of her ambitious proposals.

But on that day, I struck a nerve with an offhand remark about how little parents know about teaching their kids to read—that is, how we're just told to read to them every day and wait for the magic to set in.

"I used to get so angry when I would hear that advice," she said. "I was working so hard when my kids were little. I didn't have an hour to read to them every night and I felt so bad about it." She recalled hoping at the time that enrolling the kids in "good schools" would make up for the deficit in reading to them. Still, she had carried guilt about it for years. Her kids were in high school by the time I met her, but the memory pained her. She may have given her kids her all, but in her mind, she'd come up short on that one measure, and she didn't let herself forget it.

I've been a part of countless conversations about raising readers, and these tend to get emotional. I've heard the heartfelt testimony of a woman who records incarcerated mothers reading picture books and then ships the books and recordings to their kids, so they can have some semblance of a bedtime ritual with Mom. I've heard from multilingual parents who fret about passing on their first language without undermining their child's progress in learning English. I've spoken with parents after they've just received the jarring news that their child has been diagnosed with dyslexia. They all grappled with intense worry and frustration that came from discovering their children had a need they didn't know how to meet. You can hear the edge of panic in their tones.

The café conversation stuck with me, though, because the angst this parent was feeling wasn't coming from an overtly vulnerable position. The family wasn't in crisis. Her kids had performed well in school and were on the cusp of launching into college. Theirs was an educational success story, judged by most standards but her own.

Around the same time, I spoke with another mom who said she *had* made time to read to her three sons at length every night for more than a decade. Yet she was just as tortured by her decision to go all in on bedtime stories as the mom who hadn't. The second mom had clung to the nighttime ritual like a badge of honor, but her middle son still struggled with reading. He lacked the skill and motivation to read well for himself and had recently bombed his state achievement test.

"But I read to him every night," she told me, expressing her sense that she'd been cheated out of an expected return. She was angry that she'd have to pay a tutor to teach what he'd missed, that she hadn't acted earlier on signs that he needed more support, that what worked for one child didn't work for all. "I noticed he read like a robot, but thought it just takes some kids longer."

How could it be that moms at both ends of the spectrum—one who had read every night and one who hadn't—both described nearly identical feelings of inadequacy, uncertainty, and disappointment? The answer, I came to understand, was in the singular focus on bedtime reading. Both clung to the particular raise-a-reader tactic as *the* measure of their influence. And both suffered for it. That's because our loud cultural push for daily reading aloud, devoid of proper context, has a way of both shaming those who can't instill the habit and giving a false sense of security to those who can.

Both moms had fixated on a storytime-to-success message that resounds in the press, libraries, schools, and parenting programs. The well-intended advice is everywhere, but its delivery tends to raise more questions than it answers. Like most fairy tales, this particular story is well-worn, fractured with each retelling, and prone to magical leaps. It skips over crucial detail about the long, winding roads to reading. Day-to-day life with little kids exposes the missing plot points: How do you make family reading a habit? And if you do, does the ritual really bring about the host of benefits it's been praised for? What else is required of parents to get the job done?

A news website warns, "Children who were read five books a day starting at birth were exposed to 1.4 million more words than kids who aren't read to . . . and this reading gap may have a profound impact on a child's future literacy and vocabulary." Real-world parents wonder how short those five books may be, and how fast those parents read.

A grocery chain's book drive reminds shoppers that "the single most significant factor influencing a child's early educational success is an introduction to books and being read to at home prior to beginning school." The pressure's on, and shoppers with toddlers in tow worry about what exactly qualifies as "an introduction" and how far before kindergarten we're talking.

An author declares, "The rewards of early reading are astonishingly meaningful: toddlers who have lots of stories read to them turn into children who are more likely to enjoy strong relationships, sharper focus, and greater emotional resilience and self-mastery. The evidence has become so overwhelming that social scientists now consider read-aloud time one of the most important indicators of a child's prospects in life." Our antennae go up. *Bedtime stories do all that?*

We get the message: Reading aloud is a multivitamin for kids and a proxy for good parenting, too. If you do it each night, you can build their brains and inspire a lifetime of literary delight, family bonding, and accomplishment.

Of course, there's more to the story. Reading aloud, though valuable, isn't everything. It's time to move beyond fairy tales and to root your own reading story in reality.

The Top Six Parent Levers for Literacy

When it comes to getting kids off to a strong start, parents are in the driver's seat, but it's like one of those dual-control driving-school cars with two steering wheels, accelerators, and brakes—one set for the student and one for the instructor. Even babies who haven't spoken a word are actively learning and growing. You're not pouring information into an empty vessel. You're responding to your child's gaze, gestures, vocalizations, and (eventually) words, and stimulating more.

A time will come when you hand over the keys, take a back seat, or exit the car altogether. But initially you're in it together, and you've got a great deal of learning to do yourself about how to encourage, teach, and advocate for your child. You know how to read, but you've still got to learn how to explain how all the buttons and levers work so you can help your child use them, too. You've also got to keep scanning the horizon to see how their current language environment and experiences will impact their future success—insights that are possible thanks to advances in experimental studies, brain imaging, and more. With this vision in place, you'll be better equipped to nurture their literacy, years before they can be expected to distinguish letters or sounds, let alone read words or paragraphs.

As pediatric surgeon and early-language advocate Dana Suskind writes, "Without a concerted look, we might actually believe that the problems we see in older children start at the moment we observe them." In fact, research shows vast cognitive function disparities between infants as young as 9 months old, and sizable vocabulary and wide real-time language processing gaps are evident among toddlers.

There are countless ways a parent can make a difference early on, but the following six are the most powerful to leverage as infants and toddlers grow into preschoolers and kindergartners. I introduce them here and then revisit them in depth in subsequent chapters, so you have several sample practices, talking points, and tips to test-drive for yourself.

Lever #1: Conversation

Early talk is our point of greatest leverage for improving children's futures.

—LENA

Want your child's IQ and academic performance to land off the charts? Then launch their learning and language development with lots of conversation when they're young. I can't emphasize this finding enough: kids who engage in more back-and-forth dialogue with adults in their early years tend to have better reasoning, logic, problem-solving abilities, verbal comprehension, and vocabulary skills than kids who've experienced fewer "conversational turns" during the pivotal time frame. Simply put, conversation spurs brain development that's crucial for all kinds of success.

LENA, a national nonprofit focused on enhancing early-language experiences, created technology that's collected tens of thousands of daylong recordings of children, families, and caregivers talking in their natural home and childcare environments. Analysis of that data reveals that the *dynamism* of the conversation—how much the child participates and responds—matters, not merely the number of words spoken to or by them.

Research by a team at Harvard University, MIT, and the University of Pennsylvania gives some insight into *how* verbal exchanges work their brain magic to boost language skills, cognitive capacity, and academic achievement down the road. Using functional MRI technology, researchers found that the more conversational exchanges or turns children had experienced with adults, the greater the activity in the brain region associated with speech production, called Broca's area, during a story-listening task. In another study by some of the same researchers, diffusion MRI neuroimaging revealed that the back-and-forth of the adult-child conversation changes the *physical structure* of the brain by forging stronger links between Broca's area and Wernicke's area, a region associated with language comprehension.

For parents, these peeks into brain function and structure help explain some of the differences we see in kids' language development. They also suggest that engaging in conversation with your child from day one is a powerful way to promote optimal brain development. (Easier said than done in the age of the smartphone, when text messages, social media, and electronic notifications drive parents to chronic distraction.)

Every parent needs to know that *language* precedes literacy development.[*] Yet 94 percent of moms in one study said that no health professional had ever talked with them about their newborn's language development. Rather, the doctors and nurses who advise us often focus on immediate matters of safety.

When I brought my daughter home from the hospital, I was in survival mode, consumed with worry about car seat safety and breast milk supply. I needed to get her home and keep her fed. A few days in, more confident about the bare essentials, I started reading to her. But no one told me the specifics of how to talk to her or the urgency of why. I didn't grasp my full power to build her brain and boost her emergent communication skills through words and responsiveness. Now I know that early-childhood language affects life prospects—and so do you.

In Chapter 6, we'll explore early-language research, plus the simplest proven ways to implement its recommendations. We all bring different cultural, familial, and individual preferences to how (and how much) we talk, but most of us could stand to converse much more with our kids. Hang on to this insight and give kids the benefit of your words, warmth, and responsiveness.

---

[*] The path to reading is different for deaf and hard-of-hearing children who lack full access to the sounds of spoken language, but the foundational importance of language remains for them as well. For deaf children, overall language ability is a stronger predictor of reading skill. American Sign Language, which has its own syntax and grammar, unrelated to those of English, is the primary language of many deaf and hard-of-hearing children. And early access to sign language seems to help literacy development. Skilled deaf signers are often better readers than deaf individuals who are not proficient in sign language.

Even on the busiest, most exhausting, distracting, and turbulent days, remember the urgency of using your voice and your ears to tune into your little one.

Lever #2: Book Sharing

Books are meat and medicine
and flame and flight and flower,
steel, stitch, cloud and clout,
and drumbeats on the air.

—GWENDOLYN BROOKS

Reading out loud didn't get a reputation as "the single most important activity for helping children become literate" for nothing. It *is* pivotal for boosting brain capacity, stimulating language development, spurring vocabulary growth, increasing knowledge about the world, driving kids' motivation to read on their own, and more. It's just not the be-all and end-all. Parents need to know that there's more to raising a reader than reading aloud *and* that there's more to reading aloud than reciting words on the page.

Children have so much to learn in the first years of life, and sharing books is a powerful strategy you can use to support them. I say "sharing" books instead of "reading" them because, at first, infants and toddlers will be more interested in biting and exploring the pages of the physical book than attending to its words or letters. Plus, with young children's short attention spans in mind, you may not get to the end before they tire, wander off, or become disengaged. Your time spent sharing books with infants, toddlers, and young children should be more about togetherness, affection, and communication than reading pages word for word.

A family's literacy culture is the product of its reading resources, relationships, and rituals. Books provide stories, eye candy, and language. The parent brings experience, speech, and enthusiasm. The child engages with the book and with their parent's voice and offers attention and language of their own. The three parties—book, parent, and child—connect differently every time. Even rereadings of familiar texts are new, because our demeanor and attention changes from moment to moment, from day to day.

Over time, the books you share will introduce more complex and varied words than typical everyday speech, get your child familiar with print and spelling (as opposed to just spoken language), and build their language comprehension, to name a few benefits.

Studies show that a literature-rich home environment, exemplified by having a large home library or routine engagement with books, bolsters kids' grades and standardized test performance. One analysis found that a robust home library in childhood was associated with better literacy, numeracy, and technological problem-solving skills well into adulthood—beyond the benefits that come from parents' educational levels or career accomplishments. And those long-lasting advantages held across pooled data from more than two dozen societies spanning four continents.

As the researchers put it, "In sum, the benefits of bookishness for attainment are beyond question . . . Early exposure to books in [the] parental home matters because books are an integral part of routines and practices which enhance life-long cognitive competencies."

Many books can promote the sharing, reading, rituals, and relationships between parent and child that matter for kids' development. And Chapter 2's got you covered with specific suggestions to help you capture kids' attention at each age and stage.

Lever #3: Teaching

Just as war is "too serious a matter to be left to the generals," so, I think, the teaching of reading is too important to be left to the educators.

—RUDOLF FLESCH

Parents need to teach reading, not just model it, because (unlike with spoken language) most kids don't learn to read well without intentional, direct instruction—which many schools are ill-equipped to deliver. Witness the skyrocketing demand for private tutoring in the elementary years and the low reading-achievement scores among demographics that can't access supplemental instruction.

That said, there's good news: teaching at home can look a whole lot like play and family bonding. Home instruction needn't imitate school's approach. Caregivers have different opportunities and need different strategies than classroom teachers because we're operating in the wilds of our homes and daily lives, not in a setting marked by bells and boundaries. Effectiveness comes with matching the lesson to the child—and the moment. Depending on their age, stage, and interests, you could be teaching through song or play, reading or writing, or talking and listening.

At its core, learning to read is learning to recognize words in writing that we already understand in speech. So teaching reading has many moving parts. You need to build your child's vocabulary, highlight sounds within words, show them how letters represent speech sounds in writing, and help them sound out words. This is simpler than it sounds, especially with the tips I'll share later in this book.

Remember, you've got years for this endeavor, and daily life offers ample instructional time and opportunity. Teaching babies, for example, is conversational and relational. It's about cuddling, chatting, playing, singing, and reading. Through back-and-forth talk and attention, babies will learn to communicate via vocalizations, eye contact, and gestures. With toddlers, teaching continues to look like talking, playing, and reading together, but you get the added joy of more and more communication from your child via words, gestures, singing, scribbling, and drawing in return. When you ask questions, they answer in delightful new detail over time.

Even when it's time to get into the nitty-gritty of teaching reading, conversation remains key. You'll chat about letters. You'll bring your kids' attention to print you see. You'll use silly songs and wordplay to compare and contrast sounds (think tongue twisters and nursery rhymes). And it's important that you do, because kids entering kindergarten now are expected to know more than we were at that age.

Luckily, there are countless straightforward but powerful literacy lessons that parents can deliver easily and quickly when *we* know how. Your clarity around what you're trying to impart (alphabetic knowledge, sound awareness, vocabulary) and your thoughtful selection of a method (play, nursery rhymes, conversation) elevate everyday activity to everyday teaching. Don't worry. You'll find ample guidance in this book on how to seize teachable moments—even when you're tired, busy, and juggling other responsibilities. Chapters 5 through 9 include integrated approaches to easily teaching the reading skills that matter most.

Lever #4: Connecting

Some people think they are in community, but they are only in proximity. True community requires commitment and openness.
—DAVID SPANGLER

Roads to reading are personal. As a parent in the thick of leveraging resources for your child's benefit, you will find that the individuals you encounter often hold sway. They may share an idea, information, or invitation of significance. They may spark your child's interest or skills in unexpected ways, or step up to support you when your time, energy, or resources flag.

Consequently, part of the work you'll do to support your child will be intentionally cultivating relationships with people who have the insights and access your family needs. Here are some people who may aid your family's reading journey:

DOCTORS. Pediatricians are powerful yet overlooked allies in efforts to raise readers. Their medical training, plus their experience with hundreds or thousands of children, make them experts in child development. They're prepared to give informed answers to questions about your child's language abilities, motor skills, social development, and more. Additionally, the regular cadence of well-child visits in the first weeks and months of life provide ready-made reminders to think about your child's progress toward milestones. They're also opportunities to be vulnerable and share any concerns about your child's speech, hearing, or other development.

What's more, many pediatricians intentionally bring up kids' books during visits, because reading is truly a health matter. The American Academy of Pediatrics even issued a policy statement declaring that literacy promotion is "an essential component of primary care pediatric practice." Essential. Necessary. Vital. Crucial. Required. Not merely "nice to have." Through programs like Reach Out and Read, many pediatricians use well-child visits as opportunities to put free books in families' hands and show parents how to use them to boost kids' oral and written language exposure and stimulate optimal brain development.

TEACHERS. Hopefully, your child's teachers will facilitate vital literacy skills as well. But they can be just as valuable in identifying issues that require additional support and directing you to other professionals who can better meet your particular child's needs.

Like pediatricians, preschool teachers and early-childcare providers are vital referrers for early intervention services for developmental delays and disabilities. They can notice the signs, conduct screenings, and explore program options with families.

The same is true of elementary school teachers. I'm reminded of a rare but admirable report I read of a teacher who went side by side with a mom all the way to the level of a school-district hearing to get support for a child with learning differences.

More often I've witnessed cases where parents took offense when teachers said they couldn't fully support a particular child in class. So hear this: when a teacher tells you it's time to call in reinforcements, believe them. The limits to their resources, time, and training are real. Don't get mad; get busy finding the right person or people to meet the need.

There also are teachers who don't have the skills to help your child *and* don't have the awareness to tell you. So be proactive, curious, collaborative, and receptive, not deferential, when it comes to consulting with your child's teachers. The data shows that preschool and elementary school teachers rarely receive the literacy training they need. And parents can easily witness that teachers often lack classroom support. Getting kids reading truly requires all hands on deck, so don't be shy about asking questions (politely) and ensuring your child gets the support they need.

LIBRARIANS. A good librarian can help you find your next favorite read, but that's not all. Most children's librarians embrace a parent-education element in their work, thanks to initiatives like Every Child Ready to Read, created by the Public Library Association and the Association for Library Service to Children. They use storytime sessions and other interactions with parents to model how to ask kids stimulating questions and how to engage them in brain-building play, song, and conversation.

Increasingly, librarians also are taking on greater responsibility for directly helping kids learn to read by beefing up collections with more decodable readers and other beginning books. That means your library may be a great place to find texts that will build your child's confidence in sounding out words independently as they approach kindergarten.

Some libraries go even further. Take the Richland Library in Columbia, South Carolina. The children's section in its main branch has a dedicated space for teaching materials and offers families appointments with trained reading specialists on staff for private personalized consultations on reading strategies and interventions.

See librarians as resources beyond books, and you just might access a range of vital information, learning experiences, and activity ideas for your child and yourself.

OTHER PARENTS. Moms and dads of older children can be invaluable sources of information. They have the latest intel on the best preschools, programs, and teachers. They know intimately the specific kinds of challenges kids face as they grow. They can introduce you to resources, activities, and experiences to support your child and yourself.

Cultivating fruitful relationships with peers and experts can be easy. Inquire about their work and interests, dig into the materials and info they recommend or produce, share relevant resources with them, ask meaningful questions. Repeat. It's the ongoing touchpoints, engagement, and dialogue that turn connections into community.

Lever #5: Investing

Don't tell me where your priorities are. Show me where you spend your money and I'll tell you what they are.

—JAMES FRICK

Money talks. Or in this case, money can pay people to talk with, assess, read to, teach, and support your child. I've never seen *spending* listed in a magazine roundup of ways parents can boost reading achievement, but it is. I think it's important to say so, plainly, to parents of young children, so that they understand it's among their options when they can't meet all their child's learning needs on their own. And what parent can?

When my daughter was entering elementary school and I spoke with parents of older children about their school experiences, I was shocked by how commonplace tutoring was. One friend paid her son's teacher to tutor him over the summer, to repeat reading lessons that hadn't taken hold during the school year. Another took out a high-interest loan to cover out-of-school reading support with a national learning center.

The big supplementary educational spending wasn't limited to my little circle of friends and neighbors, though. In the decades since many of us were kids, there's been a steady rise in tutoring for young children—even preschoolers. In fact, some observers date the first "explosion in demand" for preschool tutoring to 2002 and 2003. That means more and more of today's parents were tutored as preschoolers themselves.

Industry analysts expect preschool tutoring enrollment, which has grown over the last several years, to continue to boom. All this tells us that tutoring kids before elementary school is not new, it's not limited to an overexuberant fringe of parents, and it's not going anywhere soon.

Most often, today's parents are spending on tutoring out of real concern for getting their kids ready for kindergarten or on "grade level" once they're school-aged. Should parents have to pay to secure basic literacy skills for their kids? No. Do they? Often, yes. Private tutoring is a major, long-standing player in American education with implications for how, when, and whether kids fulfill their reading potential. But it's not the only one.

Literacy spending may deserve a place among the priorities you weigh when budgeting your family's resources, alongside saving, healthcare, vacations, and so on. Beyond tutoring, well-chosen financial investment in learning evaluations, educational experiences, private schools, and high-quality childcare can drive better literacy outcomes. And don't discount smaller everyday purchases like books, field trips, and after-school activities. They also contribute to the richness of kids' vocabulary, background knowledge, and enthusiasm for learning.

Many parents make up for what they lack in money with creativity in engineering the experiences and access their child needs, meticulously tracking free-admission days at local cultural institutions and borrowing or making supplies they can't buy. Sometimes it comes down to choices like paying for a visit to a science museum versus a sports match, an enrichment class versus an amusement park. Conscious spending means recognizing the trade-offs we make every day and considering their impact.

This book focuses on free and inexpensive ways to nurture reading, and I'm a huge fan of the free books and programming that libraries provide. Still, it's important to note that how parents deploy the money they have makes an impact: spending to provide more of the language, experiences, and instruction kids need is an option.

Lever #6: Advocacy

Look at the world around you. It may seem like an immovable, implacable place. It is not. With the slightest push—in just the right place—it can be tipped.

—MALCOLM GLADWELL

When kids enter school or childcare, it becomes more obvious that our role as parents includes overseeing how well *other* people and institutions meet their needs. But raising a reader is a collaborative project from the outset. From the pediatrician we ask about developmental progress to librarians running programs we attend to the babysitters or daycare workers who watch over our little ones, we need others to nurture their learning alongside us.

Sometimes we can just request help and seek out resources, but sometimes we must push beyond that into advocacy— encouraging better support, funding, accountability, and equity for ourselves, our kids, and the broader community of children. This isn't necessarily about lobbying Congress. Advocacy comes in many forms and might look like sharing information with your child's school or teacher about the crucial importance of back-and-forth talk, monitoring the classroom video feed for evidence that the point was taken, and then scheduling a meeting if meaningful verbal engagement with the kids doesn't occur.

Some parents worry about being too pushy, and it's true that you don't want to alienate or undermine teachers with excessive demands or hover to the point of shielding your child from everyday adversity. But there's a big difference between those extremes and engaging in healthy dialogue about beneficial practices for your child and their peers. The kind of advocacy I'm talking about serves to bolster the quality of education all kids in the school or classroom are likely to receive.

This may seem uncomfortable, even extreme, but good early-childcare and education programs want engaged parents. They invite families to participate, encourage two-way communication, and welcome information about your child's particular needs and circumstances. Close family-school connections are so critical that they top the list of principles of effective family engagement generated by the National Association for the Education of Young Children (NAEYC). Specifically, NAEYC recommends that families and teachers jointly set educational goals and that families actively participate in the school community.

In fact, many parents overlook meaningful opportunities to get involved that come their way via school, childcare, and neighborhood communications. The newsletter blurb seeking volunteers for classroom or school activities presents a chance to observe how the school works and get glimpses of opportunities for change. The pamphlet offering tours of the facilities gives insight into the learning spaces your child will navigate and the occasion to ask questions about instructional needs and priorities. The strategic planning survey about the future of schools in your community invites your voice and participation, too. So take your chances to get involved—in a thoughtful, positive way.

To return to the preceding example of back-and-forth talk, a parent could ask childcare administrators to provide staff training that covers early-childhood brain development and the power of talk. They could volunteer for organizations that provide such training, make donations to those groups, or lobby for professional development resources. They could offer to fundraise to cover the costs of more training or apply for grants on behalf of the center. They could even dig into the larger policies and government funding that make high-quality care accessible or inaccessible in the first place.

The advocacy possibilities are endless (including urging better resources and more challenge for kids who aren't struggling), but it all starts with opening our eyes, ears, and mouths to discern our kids' particular needs and ensuring that they're met. We must get comfortable observing and asking questions to help us better understand reading development, recognize where our children are, and grasp what they need to foster future growth. Whoever you are and whatever your experience with school policy and curriculum, remember that your job is to bring deep care and concern for your child and all children into discussions with teachers and school officials.

You don't have to have all the answers; you just need to continue asking questions until you understand. If you don't feel confident in raising questions or taking action, seek out relatives, friends, or community members who can help you. Many cities even have organizations focused on building a healthy education ecosystem, including programs that train parents to push for positive change. Family leadership programs teach parents about education issues, including how to use community organizing and other strategies to address them.

Anyone can advocate for children, even people who don't have any or whose kids are grown, but as a parent of a young child, you bring special perspective and deep experience that can inspire and inform others to act as well. In many ways, advocacy is the culmination of the parent levers described earlier. When you do your best to cultivate your child's literacy, you will feel the limits of your efforts and have a sharper vision for what needs to change—at home, in schools, and in the community—for your child and all their peers to thrive.

Try This at Home
Journal the Journey

Power and *influence* aren't the terms most frequently associated with parenthood or early literacy. But I think they should be, because parents are difference-makers in seeding critical reading skills from day one, and as this chapter illustrates, we have a range of levers at our disposal to do that.

To fulfill your potential as your child's first teacher and best advocate, it helps to do something that teachers and advocates do—designate time and space to think and plan. Start a for-your-eyes-only journal to take note of what you've learned, what you're doing well and should continue, what needs tweaking or eliminating, and what else you'd like to investigate or try.

I'll provide prompts at the end of each chapter to point you toward things to reflect on, note, or observe along your family reading journey. If you're reading this before your child is born or while they are in infancy, just skip questions that don't apply. You can revisit and journal about them when your child grows older.

Keep the journal on your nightstand or in another visible location as a reminder to write out your thoughts, ideas, discoveries, and questions. This cumulative note-taking and reflection will be invaluable for helping you discover your strengths as a conversation partner, reader, teacher, advocate, and more. When you know where you excel, you can more consciously bring those strengths to supporting your child's development.

JOURNAL PROMPTS

- What examples have you seen of parents (including your own) pulling these six levers?

- Which levers are you using already, and which new ones will you try next? Why?

- What programs and activities could you invest in to spur your child's reading interest and skills?

- How can you expand your network of personal and professional relationships to support your child's literacy?

- What concerns or reservations do you have about your ability to use the levers?

2

The Long Run:
Language Milestones and
Literacy Targets to Watch

There are years that ask questions and years that answer.
—Zora Neale Hurston

Now that you've been introduced to the key tools available to parents, it's time to explore the road to reading from the child's perspective, from infancy through early elementary school. Remember that dual-driver car? The best instructors are attuned to what the student sees and understands so that they can patiently usher them toward greater skill and knowledge.

Let's start by setting realistic expectations. Your baby cannot read. It's not even something you should aspire to, let alone try to teach, despite the bogus claims of some products and the wishful thinking of the parents who buy them. The path to reading unfolds over the course of years, not months, and trying to shortcut the process can misdirect you from providing the critical early support and guidance that are shown to predict later reading achievement and school success.

Reading is making sense of print at a glance. More specifically, learning to read is learning to recognize *in writing* words, ideas, and concepts that we already understand in spoken language. So there are two hurdles standing between babies and reading comprehension—sufficient oral language experience and knowledge of the alphabetic code. Children must have enough back-and-forth conversation with parents, caregivers, and others to build the vocabulary, verbal reasoning, and knowledge of the world they need to make sense of words and sentences. Plus, they need direct explicit instruction in how written language works. That is, how letters and combinations of letters represent speech sounds in print. And both facets of reading—oral language and written language—take time to develop.

The parents' job in the beginning is not to teach reading but to nurture its long-term development through active attention, book sharing, and caring conversation. Think of these as your own ABCs. Do them thoughtfully and consistently from the start, and you'll create a rich early-language environment in which your child's reading can bloom. No flash cards, computer screens, or baby "curriculum" required.

In this chapter, you'll find a chronology of milestones and targets to help you anticipate the language experience, alphabetic knowledge, print awareness, and speech-sound insight that your child should accumulate as they grow into reading. By the end of this quick tour, you'll better understand how your child grows from cooer and babbler to full-fledged reader and communicator.

Many linguists believe that modern human speech abilities, including the production of contrasting vowel sounds, may have emerged millions of years ago. That span has given our brains ample time to evolve the wiring that enables even very young children to produce and understand speech in their native language with ease. Today, children's oral-language development is thought to proceed along a straightforward and predictable path with observable milestones (e.g., first coos, babbles, and spoken words). In this chapter, I will list some language developmental markers that align with norms published by organizations including the American Speech-Language-Hearing Association, the American Academy of Pediatrics, and the Centers for Disease Control. The time frames I list correspond roughly to when most monolingual children will reach the milestones, according to analysis of parent surveys, clinical and observational data, intervention and longitudinal studies, and other research.

I'll also list select *targets* related to reading skills. The ability to read a written language, in contrast to the ability to speak a language, doesn't develop effortlessly. Rather, it's a complex learned ability that emerged much more recently in human evolution with the advent of writing systems. Researchers have proposed that reading requires the "recycling" of brain networks that originally evolved for other purposes. There's incredible variation in how long it takes people to develop the oral-language foundation and absorb the written language instruction they need to learn to read well—and far too many never get there. For this reason, I use the word *target* to describe the print-focused skills. These written-language achievements and book behaviors represent the age when kids "should" have the skills or knowledge in order to meet grade-level expectations down the road—not when most kids actually do achieve these skills. In fact, most kids aren't currently meeting the targets, because there's such poor communication and infrastructure linking early care to elementary school and beyond. As a society, we've raised the bar for kindergarten readiness without properly supporting families and early caregivers in preparing kids to clear it.

Keep in mind that your family's mileage along the road to reading *will vary*. The chronology that follows isn't a standardized, validated screening tool nor a curriculum guide. It merely overviews what kids need to know and do over time where language and literacy are concerned. It's not meant to trigger a guilt trip about what you did or didn't know or do at any given point in time. If your child is older, scan the list to reflect on all that they've learned or where they might need support. Then read ahead to see what's still coming. Get on board with doing what you can *now* to move forward from where your child is, and to help them learn and accomplish what they need next for school and life.

You can also visit readingforourlives.com/milestones for more in-depth information on the language and literacy signposts described in this chapter, the research underpinning them, and ideas on what to do if you are concerned about your child's development.

May the following lists remind you of the range of skills and experiences kids need—and give you the patience and perspective to be a loving guide.

All Ears in the Third Trimester

Well, we might as well start from the top. There's evidence that initial memory and learning of voices and language begins before birth. By the third trimester of pregnancy, the sound of a mother's voice may be transmitted from the amniotic fluid through the fetus's skull and into the inner ear. So go ahead and speak up. Talk to your baby bump, because research findings indicate that exposure to ambient language in the womb likely contributes to phonetic perception.

Fun fact: there's evidence that experience with vowels affects babies' perception earlier than experience with consonants, because as researchers put it, "vowels are louder, longer in duration and carry salient prosodic information (melody, rhythm and stress)." One study of newborns in the United States and Sweden found evidence that at less than a day old, newborns distinguished between and reacted differently to vowel sounds from their native (familiar) language and another language. Why? Because they'd been hearing and getting used to vowel sounds from their native language for weeks prior.

Picture newborn babies, just 20 hours old, lying on their backs in bassinets with sensor-fitted, computer-connected pacifiers in their mouths and padded headphones next to their ears. That's how the researchers tested their hypothesis!

Birth to 6 Months

In the beginning, your newborn baby is speechless, except for a symphony of intermittent crying. They use the only sounds they know to tell you how they feel: whines of discomfort, low rumbles of hunger, and the soft moans of fatigue.

Your challenge is to tend to the immediate need—change the diaper, feed the baby, sing the lullaby—while also recognizing crying's place in a broader language, learning, and literacy journey. As children's speech and language therapist Nicola Lathey puts it, "Crying is, in fact, nature's way of enabling a baby to climb the language development ladder!" *Waaaaaah!*—those long vowel sounds are the seeds of words to come.

By the third month of life, infants add coos (comfort sounds in stress-free situations) to the mix, and win caregivers' attention and loving responses. It's easy to overlook the learning happening amid the feeding, clothing, and washing that make up newborn life. But with practice, you can tune in, and you'll be rewarded with new insights and discoveries. You'll be able to notice the precious moments when cries become more speechlike in tone, as your little one gradually gains more control of their voice. Of course, your level of talk and engagement affects your little one's, so talk and sing at every opportunity. Mealtimes, bath times, and diaper changes are perfect points in the day to make conversation.

Beyond verbal communication, a lot of language development goes on through gestures, facial expressions, and even eye gaze. Infants pay a lot of attention to and learn from what they see, including what they see you looking at. Evidence suggests that babies start following their caregivers' gaze between 2 and 4 months old—and evidence shows that they tend to learn more with gaze cues than without them.

Even though your baby won't be able to read the words, include books from day one to get yourself into a routine of talking and reading to them. By 6 months old, little ones can enjoy hearing and physically exploring books. Board or vinyl books with limited text and unadorned illustrations provide the right-fit visual and tactile stimulation your infant needs. Books with poems and nursery rhymes, too, regardless of illustrations, make it easy to use your voice in a way that will please little ears.

Start sharing books with your baby and begin discovering what they like best. Every baby is different, and yes, they have preferences. It's fun to see their reactions—reaching for the pages, pushing books away, even falling asleep. From the get-go, your baby is driving their own learning by following their interests and gathering information. Isn't that incredible?

Although some books make it easier to support your child where they are now, don't stress about picking the "perfect" first books. There are none. As literacy specialists Caroline J. Blakemore and Barbara Weston Ramirez put it, "Your choice of books is not as important as making the choice to read to your baby on a regular basis." So choosing books *you* enjoy is powerful, too.

Judge books by their shortness and sweetness at this age, not their literary merits. You're likely to hold your infant's attention on a book for only a minute or two, so you might as well make it a fun, complete experience by picking a book that delivers language and visual interest fast. And here's a pro tip that Susan Neuman, a professor of childhood and literacy education at New York University, shared with me: "Quit before they get restless. You end at the crest of the wave."

**SELECT BIRTH-TO-6-MONTH MILESTONES AND
TARGETS**

Oral Language
- Cries
- Coos
- Growls, squeals, blows raspberries, and other forms of vocal play
- Recognizes and responds to your voice

Book Behavior
- Looks at books
- Reaches for books
- Looks at print and images on pages
- Holds chin up to view pages when on tummy
- Prefers to look at higher-contrast images and human faces

6 to 12 Months

The language-learning journey continues in the latter half of the first year, through back-and-forth exchanges between you and your baby. By this age, babies may respond to simple requests like *Come here* imitate your speech, and shake their head no. They explore the world around them by gazing at and reaching for things, then passing the objects from hand to hand or hand to mouth. They're also getting more active in telling you what they think. They make sounds in response to the sounds they hear and to express pleasure or discontentment. They answer to their names, look where you point, and point at things themselves.

One study found that when infants coordinated their gaze to a caregiver's face while gesturing or vocalizing, the caregivers were more likely to respond. And how responsive caregivers were to infants' gaze-coordinated vocalizations was the best predictor of expressive vocabulary development up to 2 years old.

And now, believe it or not, is prime time to make read-alouds interactive. One study found evidence that when moms directed more questions to their 10-month-olds while reading stories, their children had better expressive and receptive language skills at 18 months old than children whose mothers had directed fewer questions to them. (Sorry, no dads were included in this research.) The toddlers who'd been peppered with questions like *What's that? Where's the doggie? Do you wanna turn the pages? Ready?* during storytime as babies showed a greater ability to understand what others said to them. They also showed a higher capacity to communicate their needs, thoughts, and ideas using words, phrases, and gestures. So there's value in reading books and asking related questions, even before kids can answer fully.

Think of books as tools for connection at this age. Play peek-aboo with them. Point and name things on their pages. And don't be alarmed if little ones chew or throw them. That's learning, too. Book sharing at this age can help kids gain fine motor skills and learn language, background knowledge, print concepts, new words, and more. Along the way, remember they're still babies and be attentive to their cues for whether to read more or take a break. Responsiveness is key.

SELECT 6-TO-12-MONTH MILESTONES AND TARGETS

Oral Language

- Babbles with long and short strings of consonant-vowel combinations e.g., *babababa*
- Babbles may mirror the rising and falling intonation of caregiver questions
- Uses sounds and gestures to capture your attention
- Turns toward sounds
- Recognizes their own name

Book Behavior

- Grasps books using their thumbs
- Pats, strokes, scratches, and chews books
- Moves books from hand to hand
- Directs their eye gaze to large, bright, and/or high-contrast pictures in books
- Points to pictures in books

12 to 24 Months

Kids in this age range aren't babies but haven't fully grown into the mobility, speech, and expression we often associate with toddlers yet, either. Susie Allison, creator of the popular BusyToddler Instagram account, proposes *taby* (to rhyme with *baby*) as the name for this group that has "all the ideas of a toddler but none of the motor skills to make it happen."

Indeed, these kiddos are stacking blocks, pouring sand and water, nesting cups, and hustling to combine a lot of different skills. Meantime, they're grasping for the words they need to express themselves, too. One year in and children are beginning to speak: *mama, dada, uh-oh*, and the like. After 18 months, kids are often talking like crazy and learning several new words a day, so their spoken vocabulary usually takes off. By 24 months, kids' vocabularies typically have doubled in size, and most will begin pairing words to create two-word phrases and sentences, such as *want ball* and *car go*. The average 24-month-old hasn't mastered all the prepositions and "glue" words, but they are communicating with clarity and directness. They can point to the pictures and objects you say or that they see in a book. They can name people close to them and some body parts.

Whatever their vocabulary size, keep treating and responding to any speechlike (non-cry, non-digestive) sounds coming from your child as genuine talk. When you respond within five seconds, there's strong evidence that those conversational turns may help bolster your little one's brain connectivity and brain function now, as well as their language skills and IQ scores down the road.

Gestures come into play in a bigger way now, too. One-year-olds are already doing some pretty sophisticated coordination of their sounds, gestures, and eye gaze to get your attention. Kids in this age range also shake their heads yes and no and use their arms to signal *pick me up* or *hand me that*.

Your little one may even start following your directions to pick up toys or point to an object they want. You can name things in books and ask them to point at them. They may make sense of longer questions from you: *Where are Daddy's keys?* They'll also start asking parents a lot of questions, too: *What's that?*

All this early speech and vocabulary learning is critical for later reading, because for an emergent reader to make sense of a word in print, they need to have heard it before. (Or, usually, many times before.) Selecting books that reflect daily life deepen the learning at this age. Little narratives about kids playing, putting on clothes, or having breakfast may pique your toddler's interest. You can even make your own books featuring pictures of friends, family, and familiar places. When you make it personal, they'll pay attention.

SELECT 12-TO-24-MONTH MILESTONES AND TARGETS

Oral Language
- Puts two words together, like *go inside* and *more water*
- Uses possessives, like *my ball* and *Mommy's cup*
- Follows directions like *come here* or *give me the toy*
- Understands and uses words for some familiar objects, actions, and people
- Uses long strings of sounds, syllables, and real words with speech-like inflection

Book Behavior
- Picks up, holds, and walks with books
- Turns pages in board books
- Enjoys being read to
- Recognizes the covers of familiar books
- Points to and names familiar characters and objects in books
- Points to things they want you to name
- Looks at pictures when the object or person in them is named

2 to 3 Years

Kids may say up to three hundred words and understand even more by 3 years old. Counting aloud while pointing out objects is now a possibility, as are maneuvering puzzle pieces into place and climbing to reach things. Play gets more social. Little ones start watching and copying what their playmates are doing and may even (gasp!) share their toys a bit.

More verbs (*run, walk, fall, jump*) and more names for places and things (*house, park, cake*) emerge now, although longer words with more syllables and consonant clusters may still get clipped. An avocado may just be a *cado,* a banana a *nana,* a squirrel a *skirl.* One helpful habit to shore up now is affirming and acknowledging whatever communication attempt they make. *Yes, that is an avocado! Yes, it's a banana! Yes, that's a squirrel!* Whatever they say can be followed with *yes,* plus a word and correct pronunciation of your own.

At this point, your little one's conceptual understanding may be taking off. Kids this age often comprehend time and position (*today, tomorrow, in, on,* and *under*) and are full of questions, especially *why.* You have an opportunity here to step up your teaching in two big ways: explaining what words mean *and* nudging your toddler to use the words, too. You can facilitate this learning just by naming the foods you eat, the clothes you put on, and the objects in your environment, as well as adding in some descriptive terms to support their word knowledge. The *cold* water, the *rough* sandpaper, the *soft* pillow.

In choosing and sharing books, keep in mind that while there's a time and place for longer children's literature, you shouldn't overlook the power of five-minute stories read on a regular basis. It's not the length of the story but the cumulative impact of engaging with you, print, and oral language that enriches a child's life and skills. Many parents learn to love short, colorful books because they can read them in a minute. Knowing that you can make an impact in a minimal amount of time may give you the nudge you need to read to your little one in the moment, versus putting it off in the hope of finding the "perfect" time.

Once you get started, you can always do repeated readings of the same books (toddlers love and benefit from repetition) or read multiple short stories to extend reading time. You just need to get started.

SELECT 2-TO-3-YEAR MILESTONES AND TARGETS

Oral Language

- Uses three-word phrases or sentences, like *Sam is running.*
- Says their name when asked
- Asks and answers *who, what, where, why,* and *how* questions
- Engages in two or more back-and-forth exchanges in conversations
- Uses some *-s, -ed,* and *-ing* word endings

Speech-Sound Awareness

- Hears and produces rhymes and alliteration
- Claps syllables
- Blends syllables verbally, e.g., *cup* plus *cake* equals *cupcake*

Print Awareness
- Recognizes logos in the environment, e.g., McDonald's
- Identifies a letter or letters in their own name

Emergent Writing
- Scribbles with intentional circles and dots

Book Behavior
- Turns book pages
- Enjoys looking at books independently
- Pretends to read familiar books
- Recalls book characters and straightforward storylines
- Points to and discusses pictures in books

3 to 4 Years

Kids' spoken language typically is quite developed at this point. Even total strangers can follow what they're saying. They're full-on conversational partners, who answer questions, respond to requests, and speak up if they feel cut off (*It's my turn!*). Feelings and everyday life become regular topics of conversation now that they have the vocabulary to support it.

Their attention to and interest in longer stories takes off, and they can show off their comprehension by answering questions about what they just heard. They're speaking in longer sentences and linking the ideas in those sentences together. They can follow (and appreciate) a clear storyline from beginning to middle to end. You can ask questions during read-alouds that prompt them to think more, guess what will come next, and connect stories to their own experiences. What fun!

You'll want to stick more closely to the text as printed on the page now, too, if you were prone to freestyling or skipping passages to keep their interest. Making speech-to-print connections is on their horizon, so the verbal-written match should be more consistent. Also, be sure to read nonfiction titles, too, which grab kids' attention, pique their curiosity, and build their vocabularies.

If books and reading aloud have been a part of your family life since your child's infancy, they may already recognize some letters, such as their own first initial. Begin gradually, yet intentionally, calling attention to more letters at this age—in isolation, in your daily environment, and in the books you read. Point to letters, name them, and describe their lines, dots, and curves.

SELECT 3-TO-4-YEAR MILESTONES

Oral Language

- Speaks clearly and forms four-word sentences, like *Mommy is eating breakfast.*
- Uses more pronouns: *they, us, hers, his, them, her, my, me, mine, you*
- Uses possessives: *dog's toy*
- Talks about objects and their functions
- Can share something that happened earlier in the day
- Identifies some colors, shapes, and letters
- Follows multistep directions, like *Put on your pajamas, brush your teeth, and then get in bed.*

Speech-Sound Awareness

- Identifies, claps, and counts syllables in words

- Identifies and produces rhymes
- Identifies and produces alliteration
- Isolates and compares initial letter sounds in words

Print Awareness
- Recognizes print in their environment
- Recognizes their own name in print, plus some familiar words
- Names letters on everyday objects, signs, and posters

Emergent Writing
- Makes letter-like scribbles to represent words
- Attempts to print their own name

Book Behavior
- Follows the structure of a story
- Makes predictions about what will happen next in a tale
- Connects text to personal experience
- Points to print as the source of information in a story
- Recognizes and prefers favorite characters in books

4 to 5 Years

Little ones at this point typically can introduce themselves with first name and last, sing a song or nursery rhyme by heart, and tell a story of their own. Ideally, 4-year-olds are also well aware of cause and effect and have developed a good bit of sophistication around language and books. They begin comparing and contrasting favorite characters in different books. They come to see books as sources for answers to questions about the world, like *What are clouds?* and *Why does it rain?*

It's time to build some print awareness by talking to your child about how books work, how print conveys meaning, and what words look like. These are vital lessons, because before a child can read print, they must notice it. Sprinkle in a few comments (max) before or during reading that direct your child's attention to how books are organized and how print mirrors spoken language. Use your finger to point to letters and words, which helps them connect the marks on the page with the speech they hear and understand.

SELECT 4-TO-5-YEAR MILESTONES AND TARGETS

Oral Language

- Uses four-word sentences, like *Look at the dog*.
- Uses thousands of words and carries on conversations
- Asks *wh-* questions: *why, where, what, when, who*
- Answers *why, how,* and *would you* questions
- Refers to quantities
- Uses conjunctions, like *when, so, if, because*

Speech-Sound Awareness

- Recognizes sounds that match and words that begin or end with the same sounds
- Recognizes and produces rhyming words
- Distinguishes, blends, and segments separate syllables in spoken words
- Recognizes single sounds and combinations of sounds

Print Awareness

- Understands that print carries meaning
- Knows print is used for many purposes

Alphabetic Knowledge
- Distinguishes letters from other symbols
- Identifies their own name in print
- Names 15 to 26 uppercase and lowercase letters
- Identifies similarities and differences among letters

Emergent Writing
- Forms letters
- Writes their own name

Book Behavior
- Holds and handles books correctly
- Listens to longer stories
- Retells familiar stories
- Points to and names words or letters of interest in text

5 to 7 Years

By 6 years old, kids typically speak clearly, tell stories with complete sentences, use the future tense, and say their own full name and address. They can count past ten, draw a person with several body parts, and copy triangles and other shapes. They also know a good deal about everyday life, from food to money.

But real differences in their literacy skills become obvious (to them and us) at this point, too. Elementary school classrooms often put reading and writing on display in ways that can't help but highlight student variations. Everything from the reading group they're placed in to the work displayed on the bulletin board exposes the differences.

It can be agonizing for parents to hear about the social drama playing out in the name of education—tales of one child being put "on the computer" because they can't read, another checking out the same baby book from the classroom library every day because that's what's on "their level," and yet another signing their name with a scribble that's different every time.

Yet all these kids are on their own unique paths to reading. We just need to clearly identify where they are, so that we can deliver the right experiences, lessons, and tools to keep them forging ahead. A few quick definitions, based on what science reveals about how beginners learn to read words in and out of context, will help.

- **Prereaders** rely mainly on visuals and context clues to make sense of words. They may recognize a word within the context of a logo—say, *Nike* or *Target*— but they are unable to read those same words in plain type without the contextual clues of color or location. They do not yet use letter-sound cues to read or write.

- **Beginning or emergent readers**, sometimes called partial alphabetic readers, are *beginning* to apply what they know about letters and sounds to read and write. They show some knowledge of how letters map to sounds but can't yet decode unfamiliar words. They spell phonetically (*duz* for *does*, for example).

- **Readers** have full command of letter-sound correspondences, can decode unfamiliar words, and can spell from memory. They've forged a solid knowledge of the spellings, pronunciations, and meanings of many words through deep experience of hearing, saying, spelling, and understanding them.

SELECT 5-TO-7-YEAR MILESTONES AND TARGETS

Oral Language

- Retells stories in sequential order
- Talks about events
- Uses a range of adverbs and adjectives
- Asks and answers complex questions
- Gives directions

Speech-Sound Awareness

- Isolates, identifies, and categorizes individual speech sounds
- Blends individual speech sounds
- Segments individual speech sounds
- Deletes, adds, and substitutes individual speech sounds

Print Awareness

- Tracks print from left to right

Alphabetic Knowledge

- Recognizes an increasing number of uppercase and lowercase letters
- Produces letter forms in writing or with materials like Play-Doh
- Matches uppercase and lowercase letters

Emergent Writing

- Writes full name
- Organizes writing from left to right

Phonics/Spelling
- Connects letters to their sounds
- Sounds out words
- Spells phonetically
- Reads and writes simple sentences
- Correctly spells frequently used words

Book Behavior
- Reads independently

Fluent Reading and Deep Comprehension at Any Age

The ultimate level of reading we're aiming for is a moving target. The sophistication your child will need to thrive will depend on the individual goals they pursue in higher education, the demands of the workplaces they enter, and the invention of new technologies and media that we can't even imagine today.

The term *literacy* itself changes over time. From the dawn of tablets (stone, that is) millennia ago to the global proliferation of the electronic variety today, social and technological change has altered the very definition of the word. As parents, we need to be aware of literacy's dynamism as modes of communication change. I think of how my daughter's second-grade year was dramatically altered by COVID-19 stay-at-home orders and an influx of digital technology. A kid who'd had limited screen time suddenly spent *hours* online daily and became adept at classroom tech, videoconferencing, and ebook procurement—because she had to. The terms of engagement with her school, teacher, and classmates had been transformed in an instant. A pandemic raised educational stakes by activating new approaches to technology, communication, and learning.

The need to leverage skilled reading to meet contemporary needs endures. And the best readers, whether 8 or 80 years old, will be defined by their ability to identify the vast majority of words in any text they encounter and construct meaning from them, individually and collectively.

As each age and stage illustrates, this level of comprehension is built on the foundation of a stimulated brain, a robust vocabulary, wide-ranging exposure to writing, and explicit instruction in the alphabetic code. To read well may take a lifetime, but it all starts from day one with the language- and literacy-building experiences parents create.

JOURNAL PROMPTS

- What's the difference between a milestone and a target? Why does the distinction matter?

- How can you use milestones and targets to better understand your child's reading journey?

- How do you currently practice the ABCs of early-language development (attention, book sharing, and caring conversation)? How, when, and where would you like to do more?

- Which area do you feel most confident in now, and which would you like to focus on more?

3

You're Hired: Essential Lessons Every Parent Can— and Should—Give Kids

Whatever the intellectual quality of the education given our children, it is vital that it include elements of love and compassion, for nothing guarantees that knowledge alone will be truly useful to human beings.

—His Holiness the Fourteenth Dalai Lama

Humans have been reading at least since the late fourth millennium BCE, when pictographic script was first etched into clay tablets with the original stylus, a writing tool sharp enough to leave an impression. And explicit reading instruction in English— directly teaching the links between letters and sounds—has been going on since the sixteenth century. But it's just been in the last several decades that we've had the benefit of rigorous experiments, massive data sets, and targeted technologies to illuminate how kids learn to read and how critical parents are in helping. Perhaps this new knowledge can push us from literacy for the elite to literacy for all.

In this chapter, we'll explore six prereading and early-reading subject areas that parents are especially well equipped to teach kids with love and lightness in daily life. They include oral language, speech-sound awareness, and letter-knowledge skills that research shows are critically important for later reading skills. Plus, we'll cover the simple work of familiarizing kids with books and print, as well as the more advanced work of matching letters to sounds (and sounds to letters).

Although abilities like these tend to show up in preschool and kindergarten screenings, they apply to a much wider age span—I'd say from birth to 116, given the remarkable story of a woman named Mary Walker, born in 1848.

Walker's dream of literacy, beautifully told in Rita Lorraine Hubbard's picture book *The Oldest Student: How Mary Walker Learned to Read*, was deferred through slavery and sharecropping, through the lives of two husbands and three sons, and the administrations of twenty-six presidents of the United States. She learned at last at 116 years old and read until her death at age 121 on December 1, 1969.

"She studied the alphabet until her eyes watered," Hubbard wrote. "She memorized the sounds each letter made and practiced writing her name so many times that her fingers cramped . . . She studied and studied, until books and pages and letters and words swirled in her head while she slept. One fine day Mary's hard work paid off. She could read!"

Literacy is still deferred for too long for too many, for lack of a strong foundation. I know a high school literacy coach whose job is to give teachers strategies to help teenagers *who can't read* to make sense of the science, math, social studies, and other lessons they receive at school. Imagine being expected to learn advanced content with no understanding of the printed information in textbooks and classroom materials. When she can, the coach pulls students out of class to tutor them in the basics of letter-sound associations that they never mastered in elementary or middle school. It's not a service she expected to provide high schoolers, but one they desperately need. And who will be there to help them when they struggle after they graduate—or drop out?

Would-be readers of any age must master the basics. There are areas of study that just cannot be skipped. Here are six knowledge areas that learners of any age can visit, revisit, and master to become more successful readers, plus ways parents can build and reinforce each.

Oral Language

Spoken words are the precursor of all precursors to reading. When learning to read, a child can't make sense of a word in print that they haven't heard and understood before out loud. So parents must carry on conversations from the beginning to build up kids' word banks. Research provides evidence that the better children's vocabularies are at kindergarten entry, the better their reading comprehension in third grade—and the better their third-grade reading skills, the higher their likelihood of graduating from high school. Whatever your child's age, they'll benefit from more conversation with you.

For optimal brain development, aim for forty conversational turns per hour when you're with your little one. It counts as a turn whenever you greet one of your baby's coos, babbles, words, or sentences with a verbal response (or they verbally respond to your words) within five seconds. It's tough to get an exact count, of course, without feedback from a "talk pedometer" like those used by researchers. Just know that most parents speak a lot less than they should—and a lot less than they think they do. The lesson here is: You can deepen your bond with your child and give them the best shot at better vocabulary by taking every conversational turn you can. Chapters 5 and 6 delve more deeply into this topic.

Sound Awareness

If knowing the power of back-and-forth talk is overlooked-parent-priority number one, then understanding that kids must learn to discern speech sounds within words is a close second. As experienced, fluent readers, we've taught ourselves to distinguish individual words and sounds that in fact don't exist as distinctly when spoken. If someone says *I hear a symphony*, we think we hear four words, six syllables, and twelve or more sounds. But that's an understanding we've layered over a continuous stream of speech that a child might hear as simply *Ihearasymphony*. The sounds within words and the words themselves often run together with no clear boundaries between one and the next.

In everyday conversation, kids are listening for meaning. There's no reason for them to pay attention to the blending, blurring, and clustering of vowel and consonant sounds *within* the words. Analysis of the sound structure of words, called *phonological awareness* by researchers, is valuable only for learning to read—but it's vital for that. In particular, research provides evidence that kids' ability to parse words at the individual speech-sound level (the subset of phonological awareness known as *phonemic awareness*) is closely related to early growth in word-reading skills. Kids who don't grasp that letters represent segments of speech and who can't discern the sounds are most at risk of reading failure.

It's a wonder that something so critical for reading doesn't garner more attention. Now that you're in the know, though, you can intentionally emphasize the sounds and rhythms of English to help your child notice them. Just keep in mind that more than listening is required for kids to get it. They need you to create opportunities for them to compare and contrast sounds in words. For example, you can bring attention to the sound structure of words in the preschool years with casual prompts like *Do the words* cup *and* pup *rhyme? Do the words* cup *and* cake *start with the same sound?*

But don't let the simplicity of the lessons fool you—the stakes are high. A 5-year-old who can't clap out the syllables in a word, blend together a few sounds, or tell you that *apple* starts with an /a/ sound will have trouble in school. Yet few parents know what specific sound-recognition skills they should be building when kids are 2, 3, and 4 years old—or how—though some stumble upon the right path just by reading and reciting age-old rhymes and tongue twisters. (See Chapter 7 to find out more.) As a mom who'd spent a fortune on reading tutoring for her young son lamented to me, too often parents hear about learning targets only after their children have missed them.

Print Awareness

Books are a handy tool for teaching an abstract concept—that the lines and curves kids see printed on paper, on products, and on signs mean something. Reading together with children presents a great opportunity to bring their attention to letters, words, and the conventions around how they are used. With just our voices and pointer fingers, we can teach the names and roles of key book features (such as author and title) and the direction we read English text (left to right, top to bottom). And it's important that we do so with preschool-aged children because researchers have found evidence for a causal relationship between kids' increased contact with print and their reading, spelling, and comprehension skills two years later.

Teaching about print is easy and should be conversational. It's your closeness with your child and your shared attention on the page that makes the lessons stick. You can use phrases like the following as you lift the cover of a book, turn the pages, and point to relevant print features (no planning or preparation required):

- *Look at the words here on the book's cover.* (Point to the words.)

- *This is the title of the book.* (Point to the book's title.) *It says* Little Leaders: Bold Women in Black History. *What is the title of the book?*

- *The person who wrote the book is called the author. These words are the author's name.* (Point to the author's name.) *It says* Vashti Harrison.

- *This is where the bunny is talking. The bunny's words are inside this bubble.* (Point to speech bubble.)

In time, you can check your child's knowledge with questions and requests like *Where do I start reading? Show me the author's name. Point to the last line.*

Also keep in mind that you don't have to have a book in hand to draw attention to print. Colors, illustrations, and more compete for attention on picture-book pages. You might find better success teaching some elements of print in isolation. Show some love to the solo word or letter on a sheet of paper, a name on a sign, or a saying on a graphic tee. There are plenty of chances to bring letters to life by noticing, pointing out, and discussing their features and meaning with kids.

Letter Knowledge

As experienced readers, we easily overlook that letters are just arbitrary marks on paper. The collections of dots, lines, and circles could mean anything. It's a process to learn to distinguish letters from pictures. It's also a challenge to remember which letter is which. After all, lowercase b and d, for example, *are* quite similar-looking.

In one of my absolute favorite picture books, *An Inconvenient Alphabet,* author Beth Anderson explores the quirks of our letters in genius fashion. She recounts the true story of Ben Franklin's and Noah Webster's shared belief that English has letters with too many sounds (think: the /g/, /j/, and /f/ sounds that G represents in *goat, giraffe,* and *laugh*), sounds with too many letters (the /k/ sound in *chorus, kite, cat,* and *quiet*), and some letters that just aren't needed at all (the silent letters in *lamb, walk, knock,* and *give*).

Letters themselves, the twenty-six we know, plus others Franklin created that never took off, are important characters in the book. Designed to represent the sounds *aw, uh, edh, ing, ish,* and *eth,* Franklin's novel (and unpopular) letters are depicted as 3D models, carried around in a sack, and handed out for examination. When I read the book with my daughter, she anticipated objections to the new letters—they look funny, would be tough to learn, and would make old books harder to read.

I share this story to underscore the fact that letters—their names, shapes, and sounds—are wonderful subjects of study, far beyond repeated renditions of "The Alphabet Song." Pointing them out, describing their features, providing opportunities for kids to scribble or write them, and asking kids to name them or utter their sounds are all instructive. And you can set the tone of curiosity and enthusiasm that makes letter exploration fun, not rote. Chapter 8 shows you how.

Letter-to-Sound Connections (aka Phonics)

Kids need to know about letters and discern the speech sounds within words. But that's not all: they also need to be able to reliably recall which letters represent which sounds so they can decode the print they see.

High-quality comprehensive reviews across the English-speaking world, from the United States to the UK to Australia, agree: Directly teaching the relationships between letters or letter combinations and the sounds they represent (aka phonics) helps kids learn to read. Parents can take a gentle, loving approach to the topic and start simply by pointing out individual letters in books or the environment and sharing the sounds each makes— for example, *The letter A says /a/. Like in* apple. Focus on the most common sound for the letter, for example, /k/ for C as in *canvas* (not /s/ as in *census*). Think: light touches, not lecture.

Jessica Toste, an associate professor in the College of Education at the University of Texas at Austin, told me that letter sounds are so helpful to know prior to kindergarten that she gives a cheat sheet to friends with young children. Titled "What Sound?," it lists the highest-frequency letter-sound correspondences because many parents haven't isolated letter sounds in a very long time, she explains, or were never explicitly taught the sounds themselves.

The teaching routine for parents is straightforward: Point to a letter and ask, *What sound?* If the child gets it right, say, *Great work matching the letter to its sound.* If they get it wrong, give them a correction: *The letter V says /v/.* Then ask them again, *What sound?* You can make the activity playful by passing a fake microphone back and forth or asking the question in a silly voice—whatever engages your child.

WHAT SOUND?

a	/a/	apple
b	/b/	book
c	/k/	cat
d	/d/	dog
e	/e/	egg
f	/f/	fish
g	/g/	goat
h	/h/	hat
i	/i/	igloo
j	/j/	jump
k	/k/	kite
l	/l/	love
m	/m/	mouse

n	/n/	nest
o	/o/	octopus
p	/p/	pig
q	/kw/	queen
r	/r/	rabbit
s	/s/	sun
t	/t/	tiger
u	/u/	up
v	/v/	van
w	/w/	win
x	/ks/	fox
y	/y/	yarn
z	/z/	zebra

Practicing letter <u>sounds</u> as often as possible supports mastery and fluency. Focus on the highest frequency sound that each letter makes (e.g., /k/ for c, rather than /s/). Use cue words to help.

INSTRUCTIONAL ROUTINE

Place card with letter "c" on table in front of child.
Teacher: **What sound?**
Student: /k/
(Repeat with other letter sounds, out of alphabetical order. Provide multiple repetitions for short vowel sounds as students tend to need the most practice with these.)

IMMEDIATE FEEDBACK

If correct:
Right, /b/. Nice job!
What's a word that starts with /b/?

If incorrect or "I don't know":
The letter "b" makes the sound /b/. What sound? (Child repeats)
Right, /b/. Well done!

 @DrToste

Down the road, you can start helping your child look at letters, match the letters to the sounds they represent, *and* then blend the sounds together, which is what we mean when we tell early readers to "sound out" words. Kids won't have to laboriously translate letters into sounds one by one forever, just as you don't. But they do need to have this skill down pat before they can move to more fluently and rapidly recognizing words in print. Even after they're advanced, or expert, readers like you, they will continue to need the sound-to-letter blueprint to decode unfamiliar words. Always and forever. Letter-sound knowledge gives kids an indispensable tool for accessing print. Chapter 8 dives into letter names, shapes, and sounds.

Sound-to-Letter Connections (aka Spelling)

Many parents don't think about teaching spelling until lists of "irregular" and high-frequency words get sent home in their elementary schoolers' backpacks to "practice" (aka memorize) at home. But ideally, it should be on your radar long before your child is ready for spelling quizzes, or even real reading. Because, as reading expert Louisa Moats puts it, spelling is a "visible record of language processing" that clearly reveals what a child understands about word structure, speech sounds, and how letters represent sounds. By tuning into the writing your little one produces, you gain one more point of connection and understanding to nurture their development.

Encourage your young child to attempt spelling by having paper and pencils handy, as well as by incorporating writing into imaginary play or games. Their creative "spellings" will progress from scribbles to letter-like scrawls to recognizable letters and ultimately to readable words. Along the way, they'll gain valuable experience and motor skills, while also giving you a view into their understanding of speech sounds, letters, and the connections between the two. Demonstrating writing in daily life, such as when you jot down a shopping list or pen a letter to a friend and explain the reason for the writing, is also a useful lesson.

Then once your little one has learned some letter-sound correspondences, you can prompt them to analyze the sounds in words in order to write them down with letters. You might ask, *What sounds do you hear in the word* dog? *Yes, /d/ /o/, and /g/. And how do you spell the sounds you heard? What letters make those sounds? D-O-G. Yes, D-O-G spells dog.* There's not a perfect speech-to-print match for every word, but you can start to teach spelling with words that are more phonetic. Letter-sound matches are the core of our writing system, so lead with clarity before getting into irregularities. Chapter 9 covers this in depth.

"Anything that is going to cause trouble with a child's reading will show up even more dramatically in the child's spelling and writing, so it's a wonderful diagnostic tool," Moats says. "It provides very detailed insight into what children need to know, and it can also tell us when children are gaining insight and what improvements they're making in their understanding of language."

For example, if your child spells life with L-I-V, you'll know that they are hearing the three speech sounds within the word but haven't yet learned to discern the fine distinction between the /f/ and /v/ sounds, which *are* very similar. To provide practice with the sounds in this example, you could ask some questions prompting the child to speak word pairs like *fan* and *van* or *foul* and *vowel* and to listen for the difference between the two and feel the difference in how they are voiced—with and without a buzz in the vocal cord.

In this way, pondering your little one's spelling allows you to praise the phonemic awareness and letter knowledge they demonstrate while also identifying specific areas where they need more practice or instruction.

Are there other things that parents can and should do to nurture literacy? Absolutely. But these are six meaningful, life-altering, often-overlooked areas that are well within our capacity to start addressing (and yes, *teaching*) today.

———————— **JOURNAL PROMPTS** ————————

- Which of the six interrelated instructional areas (oral language, sound awareness, print awareness, letter knowledge, phonics, and spelling) do you feel most confident to teach? Why?

- Which instructional areas do you need to learn more about in order to teach your child?

- How will your engagement in nurturing language and literacy skills make your child's life better?

- What are the risks of not proactively building your child's skills?

4

Yes You Can: Five Touchstones for Parents Who Dare to Teach

Those who can, do. Those who understand, teach.

—George Bernard Shaw

Reading is taught, not caught. This phrase has been in circulation for decades, but it bears repeating with each new generation of parents, and it has never been more fully supported by compelling evidence. Learning to read is a complex, unnatural, years-long odyssey, and parents should bear no illusions that their kids will pick it up merely by watching other people read or being surrounded by books.

In previous chapters, you got a glimpse of how fascinating the twists and turns that lead to literacy are, how influential parents are in helping kids navigate them, and how early in life that power is in evidence. Now I offer five teaching tenets to carry with you. Don't worry, there are no long scripts, rigid rules, or strict protocols forthcoming. These are principles any parent can remember and apply with ease during long, busy days with young children. Some of the five you may know instinctually. Others may have never crossed your mind. All deserve to be hallmarks of the way you approach raising your reader.

These touchstones are research-backed and parent-approved. Personally, I've found that returning to these principles, even after my daughter became a strong, fluent, and independent reader, still made a difference for her, me, and our relationship. Ultimately, they are calls to be a more patient, more responsive, and more purposeful parent in every context.

May you find the same comfort, wisdom, and practical guidance in them that I did. Take them to heart. Repeat them like mantras if you like. And remember, the sooner you embrace them, the better this journey gets.

It's What You Say—*and* How You Say It

Spurring literacy development, like teaching of any kind, is about creating shared meaning between you and your little one. And that requires meeting them where they are, capturing their attention, engaging in back-and-forth exchanges, and also providing the stimulation that helps them to their next level.

Parents' choices—such as asking questions versus giving directives, introducing novel vocabulary, and arranging words and phrases in advanced ways—all affect kids' language development. But parent responsiveness plays a major role as well—for example, how reliably and enthusiastically you respond to your child's speech and actions. As Harvard pediatrics professor Jack Shonkoff puts it, "Reciprocal and dynamic interactions . . .

provide what nothing else in the world can offer—experiences that are individualized to the child's unique personality style, that build on his or her own interests, capabilities, and initiative, that shape the child's self-awareness, and that stimulate the child's growth and development."

So we must have the awareness to let a child's age and language ability affect the content *and* tenor of our speech. Studies provide evidence that infants and young toddlers, for example, benefit from conversations about the here and now, with us pointing and gesturing to label objects in our immediate surroundings or on the pages of books we're reading together. And "parentese" is the speaking style of choice. Slower, higher pitched, and more exaggerated than typical speech, it's been thought to advance infants' language learning because of the ways it simplifies the structure of language and evokes a response from babies.

With older toddlers and preschoolers, we should keep examining what we're saying and how, but update the range of things we consider. It's no longer necessary to speak at a slow pace or nearly an octave higher than normal to aid a child's language development. By 30 months, the variety and sophistication of parents' word choices may have a greater influence on kids' vocabulary growth. By 42 months, talking about things beyond the present, such as delving into memories of the past or discussions of what will happen in the future, is positively related to kids' vocabulary skills a year later.

While it's unnatural and unrealistic to monitor yourself all day, the thing to remember is that our words and responsiveness fuel powerful learning for kids. Set aside ten minutes a day of mindful communication, focusing on your little one, your words, and the interplay between them. Over time the focused practice will create habits that spill over into other conversations, too.

Learning Takes Time—and Space

We live in a catch-up culture, where people feel perpetually behind and forced to hustle near the finish line after being waylaid by hurdle after hurdle. This contributes to the (false) belief that we can make up in intensity what we lack in good pacing. But we can't cram kids' way to reading.

Ask any learning scientist about the relative merits of massing study together versus spreading it out over time. They'll tell you that spacing between sessions boosts retention of the material. The proof of the principle (known as *spaced learning, interleaving,* or *distributed practice*) shows up all over the place. Numerous studies across the human lifespan, from early childhood through the senior years, have documented its power. And there's evidence of the benefits of spaced study across a wide range of to-be-learned material, such as pictures, faces, and foreign-language vocabulary and grammar. Even learners taking CPR courses performed better if their classes were spaced apart. So if you want your child to remember what you're teaching, digging into it for ten minutes a day for three days likely will beat a half-hour deep dive. The spacing effect is among the field of psychology's most replicated findings.

Incidentally, a study found that a bias for massed learning emerges in kids in the early elementary school years, so you're in good company if spaced learning feels counterintuitive. In the preschool years, the kids were as likely to think learning something bit by bit over time was as effective as learning it in a clump. During elementary school, though, the kids started (wrongly!) predicting that massed learning would be better at promoting memory than spaced learning.

Maybe the teaching methods employed in so many classrooms give kids (and parents) the impression that repetition, repetition, repetition in one sitting is the way knowledge sticks in memory. Want to learn your spelling words? Write them over and over again in different-colored pencils. Want to practice your handwriting? Fill that page with well-formed letters.

Spacing things out may feel inefficient, but it's more effective, more fun, and a better fit for daily life with young kids. Parents have a natural advantage in teaching more gradually, because we are with our kids for hours a day over the course of years. We aren't under intense time pressure, at least over the long term, removed as we are from the confines of a school day or school year. Nor do we have to find a way to meet the needs of twenty-five kids or more at once.

And keep in mind that the lessons we give needn't be formal. Teaching young children often looks like simply being present, engaging, talking, playing, and singing. I once ordered a home spelling program that included what felt like 50 million individual magnetic letter tiles, color-coded index cards, and scripted teaching procedures. I was so tired from separating and organizing all the materials that I never got around to working through the curriculum with my daughter.

Ultimately, conversation over a few games of prefix bingo one week taught her more about prefixes, suffixes, and units of meaning within words than the elaborate curriculum did. Why? Because that was the method I enjoyed and followed through on—the one that worked within the context of our relationship and our attention spans. She loves board games; I love talking about words. Win-win.

The takeaway: Do what works for you, and do it a little at a time.

The More Personal the Lesson, the Better

Helping your child learn to read requires making decision after decision. Which letters or words to teach? Which song to sing or story to tell? When making the calls, err on the side of making the lessons themselves personally meaningful for your child. Sometimes it's as straightforward as teaching the child the letters in their name first, making up songs and stories featuring their pets, or choosing vocabulary words from their favorite books. Sometimes it's as deep as practicing fluency by reading aloud texts that affirm and sustain a child's cultural heritage or community.

To help conceptualize this, researchers have defined three levels of personal relevance, from mere *association* to *usefulness* to *identification*. When a reading lesson centers on a passage about your child's sport of choice (say, soccer), that's making a personal association. If you can make it clear how the lesson is useful for advancing a goal your child is after (like learning the training secrets of their favorite player), even better. But if you can make the activity resonate with their sense of self, you're really onto something. If your child identifies as a student of the game, for example, they'll be way more invested in seeking out information to learn more. The same dynamics are at play with younger children, too. This is what's going on when a little one named Anna sees the letter A and says, *That's my letter!* She's owning it—and identifying with it. It matters to her and she learns it quickly.

The power of personal meaning also helps explain why parents so often find that something that worked like a charm with one child falls flat with another. Kids' associations, judgments of usefulness, and identities vary widely, even when they grow up under the same roof. Locking in on what makes your individual learner tick to facilitate resonant experiences just for them is golden.

Luckily, you have a built-in feedback mechanism for determining what's working: your child. Even infants express preferences. A little one might reach for the same book with bold illustrations or lift-up flaps over and over again. You may also find that what gives the lesson meaning is *you*—your demeanor, engagement, and responsiveness can be tremendous motivators.

Praise the Process

You're voluntarily reading a parenting book, so I'll venture that you value learning and have confidence that you'll reap some benefit from the effort you put into acting on the tips compiled here. You believe that you can know more, teach better, and make an impact. And I imagine that you want your child to feel the same sense of self-assurance as they pursue their own challenges.

One way to cultivate that can-do spirit is by cheering on their hard work, focus, and determination by name. Instead of giving generic praise like *You're so smart,* say specifically what you loved about *how* they learned—not just the results. For example, if your little one is beginning to write letters you could say, *Great job picking up the pencil and writing. I see you working to hold it in your grasp.* You'll celebrate their work and lay the motivational track for other efforts to come.

Research by psychologist Carol Dweck and others has found evidence that when parents praise kids' effort in the learning process—not outcomes—it impacts their children's belief that they can improve their ability with effort. With that growth mindset, they are more likely to think they can get smarter if they work at it, a trait that boosts learning, achievement, and resilience.

In a longitudinal study, Dweck and colleagues traced the whole path of these relations, from parents uttering things like *Good job working hard!* when their kids were 1 to 3 years old, to testing those same kids' academic achievement in late elementary school. They found evidence that this process-related praise predicted a growth mindset in children, which contributed to strong performance in math and reading comprehension later on in fourth grade. The study also found evidence that parents established their praise style (more process-focused, or less so) early on. So make an effort to give meaningful compliments. You've got room to grow, too.

And here's a pro tip from Christine Reinders, a veteran teacher and reading specialist. You can build a child's vocabulary and self-regard when you phrase your praise thoughtfully. When working with young children, she likes to recognize their determination and teach new words by saying things like this: *It was very difficult trying to read that word, but you kept trying even though it was tricky. Did you do your best even though it was tricky? Yes, absolutely! That is called perseverance. You persevered! Feel proud that you tried your best, and always remember to persevere. That is an important trait.*

She says it builds confidence, reinforces risk taking, and affirms that it's okay not to be perfect when learning. Don't we all need that reminder?

When in Doubt, Look It Up

This was my dad's go-to saying when I peppered him with questions as a kid. A good reference guide, in our case a giant *Webster's* dictionary that he kept on a wooden stand in his office, was always the first stop for a spelling, definition, or example. As an adult, I find his words remain with me, reminding me how important it is to continue learning as we endeavor to teach our kids. My dad didn't have all the answers and wasn't afraid to learn alongside me.

When it comes to nurturing and teaching reading, we should stay curious and work to deepen our content knowledge, versus falling back on instructional methods that are more familiar than effective. For example, if you decide to teach spelling (and you should!), make it a priority to learn something about word origins and get a handle on conventional letter-sequence patterns.

Having a child write a word over and over again is *one method,* but it's one you'll probably feel more comfortable letting go of as you know more about *why* we spell how we do. Fear not, pointers on how to talk about words and spelling in ways that both boost your confidence and deepen your child's understanding are coming up in Chapter 9.

When we're well informed about how written English works and how reading develops, we can take advantage of the countless teachable moments in everyday life. So without further ado, the following chapters will help you learn what you need to teach with confidence.

———————— **JOURNAL PROMPTS** ————————

- Think of the conversations you've had with your child recently. What did you talk about most? How much back-and-forth did you engage in? What kind of tone did you use?

- How can you set up your physical environment to remind you to nurture literacy bit by bit, day by day? Brainstorm your own list of things to try, such as putting magnetic letters on the fridge, hanging a nursery rhyme mobile over the changing table, or posting an alphabet chart on the wall.

- What are some language and literacy skills your child is building now? How can you nurture or teach them in a way that ties into your child's interests, goals, or identity?

- What are some everyday opportunities to praise your child's actions and efforts (versus results)? Write out exactly what you could say.

- What's a topic your child may ask you about that you don't know well yourself? What's one way you can advance your knowledge to help?

5

Nourishing Words: The Lasting Impact of Early Language

Our children cannot dream unless they live, they cannot live
unless they are nourished, and who else will feed them the real
food without which their dreams will be no different from ours?
—Audre Lorde

Some time ago, I read an unusual report from the Canterbury region of New Zealand. It told, in the subdued tone of an academic journal article, the story of an urgent rescue mission. On September 4, 2010, a massive earthquake rocked the city of Christchurch (population: 350,000). The seismic event measured 7.1 in magnitude. It tripped circuit breakers at substations and knocked out power. Building facades collapsed, crushed cars, and jammed roads. And that was just the warmup. For the next year and a half, the devastation continued, with ten thousand aftershocks and three more full-blown earthquakes. A violent quake in February of the following year killed 185 people and leveled the central business district.

But the report that caught my attention wasn't about the first responders who rushed in to tend to the injured, restore power, provide water, and reopen transport. It wasn't about the elaborate emergency-management structures that launched within hours. It was about an unheralded cadre working to address another type of fallout from the earthquakes, one a lot less visible than liquefied soil sending buried pipes floating to the surface.

The rescuers I read about were psychologists, health advisors, and educators, all collaborating to pilot a program aimed at preventing a crisis they foresaw for children affected by the earthquakes. They knew that life in extreme instability, whether wrought by war or famine or natural disaster, breeds developmental difficulties and reinforces inequities, with lasting consequences. They had seen data, collected six thousand miles away in Santiago, Chile, that suggested that an earthquake can create educational aftershocks, too. Preschool kids who took early-language and early-literacy assessments shortly after the earthquake performed worse on letter-word identification and text comprehension than comparable kids who took the same assessments one year before the earthquake. The study provided evidence that their performance had been hurt by their parents' disaster-wrought stress and their own. Plus, school-entry data back in New Zealand revealed that many kids living in earthquake-affected communities struggled with expressive language and awareness of sound structure in words. The researchers who ran the pilot program summed up the nature of the challenge with characteristic understatement: "These results suggest that such experiences may impact families, with potential developmental sequelae for children."

But before vulnerable kids' development can be protected and bolstered, parents, teachers, and other concerned parties must *notice* the learning crises, which aren't glaring like abandoned buildings with missing windows and walls. Next, we have to sustain interest and intentional action through a yearslong recovery, without the benefit of construction clamor to herald our progress.

The fact is, on any given day in any given community—natural disaster or not—there are learning crises brewing. There are children who aren't getting the language they need, due to household disorder and chaos, parent disposition, and a range of other circumstances. And although poverty creates the kind of stress and instability that lessen child-focused conversation and responsiveness in homes, many well-educated and advantaged families struggle with talk, too, for any number of reasons. Across demographics, differences in language skills are associated with differences in healthcare outcomes, high school graduation rates, job placement results, earning levels, and more.

The central truth every parent must grasp is this: oral-language skills are required for reading. Just as kids crawl before they walk, they talk before they read. And before they talk, babies listen, grunt, and coo. We must facilitate and encourage it all.

As language development expert Roberta Michnick Golinkoff and colleagues put it, "Language is causally implicated in most of what children learn in the first years of life. Indeed, kindergarten language scores, which are deeply rooted in the language development of infants and toddlers, are the single best predictor of school achievement in all subjects in third and fifth grade."

Psychologists Anne E. Cunningham and Jamie Zibulsky describe the delayed strong influence of early oral-language skills and reading development as a kind of "sleeper effect." The importance of early oral-language skills should not be underestimated, they say, because "no matter how accurately a middle school student can sound out new and difficult words like *omniscient* or *prejudice*, his ability to understand these words in context will depend on how often he has talked about these words and the concepts related to them. Each new word that a child acquires verbally becomes a word that he will eventually be able to recognize and make sense of when he sees it in print, so early vocabulary development is an essential skill for later reading success."

Think back to the overlapping, interrelated language and learning processes described in Chapter 2. They are like one of those elaborate domino creations that garner millions of views on YouTube. A creator devotes weeks to meticulously placing domino after domino into an elaborate design, just to engineer a few minutes of excitement when the first block sets off a chain reaction that topples thousands more. Some tumble in a straight line. Others, placed at a slight angle, bend the pattern into curves and turns. Still others are positioned to hit two dominos at once, sending branches of the design off in different directions.

Early parent talk is the first domino. It pings (through years of back-and-forth conversation) straight into an infant's grunts, coos, babbles, and eventually words. At the same time, those early conversations knock down other dominos and create a new branch at the split that builds momentum toward a toddler's vocabulary, which affects school readiness, which predicts third-grade reading, which correlates with high school graduation, and so on.

The influence that frequent, quality parent talk has on eventual literacy is so strong and begins so early in life that many experts now rank it above the once be-all, end-all practice of reading aloud. In fact, some argue that talking with your child from infancy may be "the single strongest action you can take to increase your child's educational opportunities." Language learning starts early—in utero, by about 35 weeks gestation—and the formation of synapses involved in language learning peaks during the first six months after birth. Researchers in one study found evidence that the richness of a child's early-language environment predicts their vocabulary, their language and speech processing, and fourth-grade literacy outcomes better than their mothers' education level or family welfare status.

Words matter. Timing matters. You matter.

Language Nutrition Defined

We talk to our kids for all kinds of reasons in the moment—to soothe, to encourage, to entertain, to direct. And there's power in every word we speak, including the impromptu conversations we have while giving baths, making meals, and playing at home. But sometimes we go above and beyond, delivering a kind of fortified talk that's extra nourishing to their long-term brain, language, and social development.

Some early-language advocates call this "language nutrition" to emphasize just how vital it is. You may even have had a coaching session at the pediatrician's office, with a nurse or doctor modeling how to talk to a baby, inviting you to do the same, and then encouraging you to practice the techniques at home.

I experienced such a doctor's visit when my daughter was 3 years old, and I'll admit I found it puzzling at first. We'd just relocated to Texas and were due for a well-child appointment at a new pediatric practice. Without any preamble, the doctor locked gaze with my daughter, introduced herself, and then directed all the exam questions to Zora. I felt sidelined and devalued as a source of information about my daughter's health, but that was far from the doctor's intention. I had no way of knowing it, but in addition to giving a medical exam she was modeling rich language, another kind of prescription for a child's well-being. The doctor had just forgotten that as a new patient I needed a bit of orientation to the practice.

In Georgia, a statewide campaign called Talk With Me Baby teaches obstetric, neonatal, and pediatric nursing students to coach parents and caregivers on language nutrition in a child's first years of life. They use the *I Do. We Do. You Do.* instructional framework, which shifts from direct demonstration by the teacher to guided instruction or collaborative learning alongside the student to independent practice by the student. In the *I Do* step, nurses model how to talk with a baby by themselves directly addressing the baby, saying things like *Hi, baby! It's so good to see you. How are you feeling today?* In the *We Do* step of the protocol, the nurse invites the parent into the conversation with the baby and shares tips on why and how to talk to little ones. Finally, in the *You Do* step, the nurse passes the baton to the parent to keep up the child-directed talk and provides feedback and encouragement.

The takeaways? Your speech is an essential part of the environment your child inhabits and learns from. To make the most impact on a child's development, speak directly to them in infancy and early childhood. The quantity, variety, and responsiveness of the words you share with them influences the size of their vocabulary and the speed of its growth. Watch and listen for their communication, however subtle—a coo, a reach, a cry—and respond wholeheartedly, with words, expressions, and gestures of your own to keep the dialogue going.

Brains differ at birth, even among some twins from the same egg, who aren't 100 percent genetically identical at birth. Newborns vary widely in their processing of sights and sounds, as well as in their speed of responses to stimuli—but it's their environment that makes these differences trivial or meaningful in the long run, states Usha Goswami, director of the Centre for Neuroscience in Education at the University of Cambridge. "Usually, as long as the environment is rich enough, sufficient learning experiences enable less efficient brains to reach similar developmental end points to more efficient brains," Goswami states.

From infancy, children are active, engaged learners. They choose where to look, and they make bids for the attention of the people around them by wriggling and crying. A parent who responds by swaddling them in a blanket, handing them a toy, or empathizing with a gesture of their own nurtures the child as a person and a learner. The caregiver who makes a habit of reacting with immediacy, warmth, and words sets an incredible trajectory for cognitive, social, and emotional growth.

That's welcome news for everyone who wants to make a difference beyond the genetics you contributed to your child's makeup. Your talk and responses count significantly among the learning experiences they need. The process is verbal, but it's also interpersonal. You feed your child language within the context of your relationship. The love and meaning you share deepen the impact of your words.

Talk Like This

Beyond the quantity of words you speak, *the way* you speak them affects different aspects of your child's language and literacy development. Here are the chief characteristics of nourishing early-caregiver language and how they help kids learn:

- *Child-Directed:* Your words are delivered expressly to and for the child, as opposed to language they pick up indirectly through overheard adult conversations or media. Child-directed speech supports language learning because it provides much more than words. It pairs content with helpful physical, social, and other cues.

- *Melodic:* Your delivery is clear, high-pitched, and with more exaggerated vowels than the way you might address adults. Many moms do this naturally, even taking prosody to the point of parody. And for good reason—infants prefer listening to this "baby talk," and that attention may support their ability to discern the sounds within words as well as recognize word boundaries and grammatical units.

- *Loving:* Your words and gestures are warm, affectionate, and encouraging, versus stern commands or brusque movements. New research related to how emotion is expressed through movement suggests that by 11 months old kids can detect whether actions like grasping an item are performed with happy or angry motions—and shows that they match what they observe with happy or angry facial expressions of their own.

- *Home Language:* You speak in the language you know best, not necessarily the dominant language of your neighborhood or the school your child will attend. This is so that you can give your child the richest vocabulary, most fluent speech, and deepest background knowledge to support learning in any language.

- *Repetitive:* You use consistent names and labels for the people and things in your child's environment, so your little one gets many opportunities to distinguish among words in the stream of speech, make the connections between words, and discern word meanings. You also frame sentences with short, familiar phrases like *Look at the ___*, *That's a ___*, *Where is the ___?*, and *There's the ___*. The setup and repetition help toddlers grasp common nouns.

- *Expressive:* You point to the things you're referring to and match your facial expressions to your words. The body movements capture infant attention and give helpful context for the meaning of what you say, which boosts learning.

- *Responsive:* You listen well and provide feedback that's contingent on your little one's babbles, words, facial expressions, and gestures. This quality of interaction is predictive of kids' language achievements. You also give your little one plenty of time and space to receive what you communicate and to express themselves, too. There's evidence that by 11 months, infants coordinate their gaze, vocalizations, and gestures to intentionally communicate with caregivers. If your baby is staring at a fire truck or touching your sweater, you might say, *Oh, yes, a red fire truck.* Or, *Feel the sweater. Isn't it soft?*

The nourishment that language provides when parents and children feed one another words, attention, and contingent responses is like a holiday feast spread over many courses, punctuated with lively rounds of conversation and laughter. Unlike the dense, compact nutrition of an energy bar, it's meant to be savored.

How Reading Aloud Fortifies Talk

None of this emphasis on early talk with kids should dampen your enthusiasm for reading aloud. In fact, reading picture books to and with kids boosts their oral-language experience by introducing more (and more diverse) vocabulary. Researchers at the Ohio State University in collaboration with the Columbus Metropolitan Library estimated that kids whose parents read them five board or picture books a day would have heard 1.4 million more words during storybook reading by age 5 than children who were never or seldom read to. Other studies have found that the vocabulary within picture books is more varied, challenging, and enriching than what's typically heard in everyday family conversation.

Moreover, a particular style of book sharing, called "rich reading" by the New Zealand team that responded to the earthquake learning crisis, can encourage high-quality conversation. It's a style of reading aloud that fosters comment and discussion. The reader talks about the illustrations, labels the characters' emotions, relates the content of the story to their child's life, and generally finds ways to heighten the child's engagement with the tale, as well as the little one's awareness of the text conveying it.

Reading with babies especially is a sensory, dynamic, visceral experience, and an efficient vehicle for the back-and-forth language we're going for. Every part of the exchange is novel for the infant—the smell of the book, the feel of the pages, and the motion as you move from cover to cover. Not to mention the look of the text and images on the page, and the words, sounds, and gestures they elicit from their parent.

With so much going on, where should a parent focus during

storytime? On the relationship, I say. For the first year of your child's life, don't worry about teaching. Stay in nurture mode. Hold your baby close. Tune in to their responses. Lean in to their coos, babbles, kicks, and giggles, and return it all with as much vocabulary-rich talk as you can muster. You can't go wrong when you open a book, read, and follow the child's lead.

As your little one grows into a toddler, preschooler, and beyond, books can help them learn all kinds of things, from sound awareness and letter knowledge to story structure and science. The possibilities for meaningful, expansive conversation are endless when a well-chosen book, enthusiastic parent, and engaged child commune. Visit readingforourlives.com/books for a list of recommended reads for each age and stage.

Cultivate Mindfulness

Once we know the impact of oral language, the challenge is to live it. For me, it's helpful to think of parental speech and interaction as one dimension of the broader practice of mindfulness—consciously paying attention to the present moment. I first studied mindfulness meditation in a stress-reduction class hosted by the health center at my college. As an anxious overachiever, I was fascinated by the idea that you could experience the events of your life without being fully immersed in or carried away by them. I took a similar course a decade later, as a new mom recovering from major knee surgeries and trying to manage the pain, along with my resulting irritability. I practiced finding a sliver of perspective in any given moment and conjuring the space to create more-helpful responses to whatever life brought my way.

I studied mindfulness meditation as a strategy for high-stress, high-pressure, high-stakes situations, but I now appreciate its value in every aspect of life (and parenting). The careful observation of our own thoughts, words, and deeds gives us the consciousness we need to discern what's helpful, powerful, or useful in any moment. With that awareness, we learn to wield our words in ways that heighten kids' understanding of language's meaning and function. And, even beyond the nuts and bolts of literacy building, we gain a greater capacity to speak in ways that nurture and sustain our children as whole people. As meditation teacher Joseph Goldstein puts it, "Part of mindfulness is calling to mind or remembering what is skillful, what is unskillful . . . and so we're really developing a wisdom about ourselves, our hearts, our minds, our lives."

This perspective has profound implications. When we can observe what's constructive and what's not about our interactions with kids, we then have the option to consciously continue or discard our patterns. And even more—we have a chance to create new, more constructive ones, so that in the future we can do the good work automatically.

The Other Why

Another reason to focus on nurturing a strong oral-language environment from day one is that it's a proven stress reducer—for you. Tuning in to your baby, heightening awareness of their bids for attention, and engaging with them in back-and-forth conversations as they learn language actually reduces parenting stress, according to a study of moms who faced the typical stresses associated with childrearing *plus* household financial strain.

In this study, moms who received coaching around how to read with their kids and how to infuse more nourishing language into their routines reported levels of stress reduction typically associated with interventions explicitly designed for that purpose—things like therapy or direct instruction in coping mechanisms. Something about the practices the intervention taught took pressure off participants. It coached moms to increase sensitivity to kids' cues, reflect on parenting, and be verbally responsive. I'm not saying this kind of nourishing engagement is a cure-all, but it's comforting to know that a steady stream of thoughtful parent-child interactions can soothe your nerves a bit.

It's wise to talk about parenting stress in the context of early language and literacy learning because, while relative stress ebbs and flows, research suggests that a steep incline typically takes place in the earliest years, as kids grow from infants to toddlers. Theorists attribute this to the intensity of wrangling kids as they get more mobile, vocal, and autonomous. After that point, parenting stress seems to hold pretty steady, natural disasters and catastrophes aside.

Stress is obviously major for families experiencing homelessness, intimate-partner violence, job insecurity, and other major upheavals. But the subtler accumulation of minor stressors—the daily hassles of parenting—are important determinants of parent well-being, parent-child interactions, and child educational outcomes, too. (And, to be clear, *daily hassles* is a technical term. I've never felt more *seen* than the day I discovered the Parenting Daily Hassles Intensity Scale in the *Journal of Marriage and*

Family. The struggle, ample documentation shows, *is* real.) Routine parenting work, like feeding picky eaters, managing stockpiles of family laundry, and defusing temper tantrums, can compound into distress, depending upon how frequent and intense the demands and how near and robust our networks of support are.

Learning how to talk to and engage with your child doesn't begin to address the financial woes, job strain, time pressure, and million other challenges real families navigate, of course. But a bit of support in building (and trusting) your capacity to nurture their cognitive, social, and emotional development can lighten your load.

A global team of scientists reviewing data from a vast network of GPS monitoring systems discovered in retrospect something they'd never seen before—a gentle rocking of the earth, a "wobble," they termed it, in the months that preceded a magnitude-9 earthquake in Japan. It was caused by one of the planet's tectonic plates sliding beneath another one, jamming and tearing the earth, preparing to quake. The signs were there, but no one was looking.

Like an unnoticed wobble before an earthquake, weaknesses in early-language environments are vast yet slow-moving. They pose quiet but seismic risk to kids' long-term literacy prospects. That's why parents need to become sensors in a network aimed at noticing, and correcting for, threats to children's optimal development and literacy. We don't need the expertise of a seismologist or advanced GPS technology to get this job done. A bit of history and reading science, a lot of enthusiasm, and an openness to learning and teaching will do.

Take a long view to fully appreciate and wield your influence. Whenever you speak, you do much more than deliver a message in the moment. You are laying the groundwork for lifelong literacy.

Try This at Home
Play More, Say More

Fun, social interactions (aka play!) start in infancy and have positive impacts for both parent and child. A study of naturally occurring baby games, like peekaboo—where a parent and child share attention, gazes, facial expressions, touches, gestures, and vocalizations—showed that they were associated with a boost in the release of the feel-good hormone oxytocin.

In your child's early years, it's great to have a few go-to games in your toolkit for times when you need a conversational pick-me-up. Boost your talk and playfulness anytime, anywhere by keeping some language-rich games in your metaphorical back pocket.

I SPY ages incredibly well—with variations for babies, toddlers, and preschoolers—and it works in a variety of settings.

The game uses the phrase "I spy with my little eye something _____" to set up a hunt for an object of your choice. Start by choosing an object—say, a blue dictionary on the kitchen counter—and then give hints: *I spy with my little eye something blue*. The child looks around and (hopefully!) responds by saying they see a blue book or perhaps simply pointing. Then your child takes a turn to give you hints to find the objects they choose, giving them a wonderful chance to flex their expressive vocabulary muscles.

As your child grows, you can adapt the game to pose new challenges. With the youngest children, you might use it to draw attention to colors or shapes. Later you can amp it up to direct your child toward certain letters or rhyming words, as in *I spy something that rhymes with car. Yes, the peanut butter jar!* The possibilities are endless, but here are a few to get you started:

- Shapes: *I spy something that's square.*
- Colors: *I spy something red.*
- Letters: *I spy the letter T.*
- Letter sounds: *I spy the letter that says /s/.*
- Rhyming: *I spy something that rhymes with* stair.
- Beginning sounds: *I spy something that starts with the /k/ sound.*
- Ending sounds: *I spy something that ends with the /r/ sound.*

JOURNAL PROMPTS

- Describe the current language environment in your home. Who talks directly to your little one (e.g., parents, siblings, babysitters)? When does most of the talk happen? How much of the talk is directive, such as giving an order or instructions like *Sit down*? How much is descriptive, labeling objects or events in a book or the environment like *It's a puppy*? And how much is inquisitive, asking a question like *Where is the ball?*

• Which of the reasons to talk with your child from day one resonate with you most?

• What interferes with your ability to carry on more conversations with your little one?

• What will you do differently as a result of what you've learned about back-and-forth conversation with kids?

6

Taking Turns:
How to Make Conversation
a Habit from Day One

Every day, in a hundred small ways, our children ask, "Do you hear me? Do you see me? Do I matter?"

—L. R. Knost

For most of my life, I've held the strong opinion that people talk too much. Among the documents I found when thumbing through files from my school days is an ode to succinctness that I wrote for an English class. In the poem, I call on people to "get to the point," "keep things simple," and—presumably for the sake of the rhyme—to avoid "dangling participles." As an adult, I live for days when I don't take calls or meetings and spend a full workday reveling in silence.

So imagine my surprise as a quiet-craving person to discover that all the "let them catch you reading" stuff I'd seen on blogs and in parenting magazines was not critical for raising a reader, but making lots of conversation with babies and toddlers was. If leading reading by example alone isn't a thing, I learned, parents had best use our voices to proactively bring kids' attention to print (more on that in Chapter 8) and to build the oral vocabulary they need to make sense of words on the page.

I'm not the only parent who missed the memo about sparking meaningful conversations with kids, beginning in infancy. Studies of kids' early-language environments show enormous differences in both the quantity and quality of talk that kids engage in with their families. Parent talkativeness varies for all kinds of reasons, from our personalities, stress levels, and time demands to our beliefs about what babies understand and cultural norms about kids' proper role in conversation with adults.

As discussed in the previous chapters, all of this matters a lot for kids' literacy. It also matters because young children tend to follow their parents' lead when it comes to how much they talk as they grow older. LENA, a national nonprofit that offers early-talk technology and data-driven early-language programs, compared the average daily vocalizations for kids with parents who talked to them more (Adult Word Count [AWC] in the highest 20th percentile) with kids whose parents talked less (AWC in the lowest 20th percentile). As you can see in the following graph of kids' average daily vocalizations from LENA's Natural Language Study, talkative parents tend to have talkative little ones and taciturn parents (caregivers who say little) have taciturn kids. In Chapter 5, we explored the dramatic consequences those differences in early-language environments and early oral-language skills may have for kids' reading and learning outcomes years later.

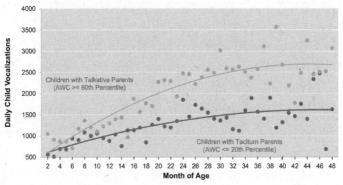

Source: LENA

This is the best illustration I've seen of the need for parents to say more to inspire kids to do the same. So now the crucial question is *how?*

The rest of this chapter offers practical strategies for instilling strong conversational rituals and routines, based on advice from people who know early talk and habit formation best. Experiment with each approach to discover the ones that make you most able *and* motivated to converse more with the kids in your life.

And to the extroverts out there, you're not off the hook. You should take heed of this advice as well, because parents of all stripes, from brusque to verbose, tend to overestimate how much they talk with their kids—and talking *at* kids isn't the same as talking *with* them.

Talk It Up

When it comes to family conversation goals, you're in luck. Our knowledge about the specifics of how talk affects brain development has skyrocketed in recent years, thanks to more than ten thousand children from birth to age 3 who have donned tiny LENA recorders in their shirt pockets for research's sake. These "talk pedometer" devices and their software are so sophisticated that they can separate talk and babbles from crying and digestive noises, record up to sixteen hours of continuous speech data, and customize analysis down to the millisecond. That processing power offers us tremendous insight into exactly how different families converse *and* how those differences tilt kids' learning trajectories.

It's a far cry from the days when researchers huddled in homes tape recording family chatter and then transcribed and coded the data by hand (for years!) to discern patterns. In contrast, the new tech and analysis deliver unprecedented scale, rigor, and details that parents need to know. As noted before, if you're aiming for optimal brain development, then at least forty conversational turns per hour is the magic number for kids 3 and younger.

The research also has something to say about how those turns happen during the early years of intensive caregiving for babies and toddlers when hours are spent holding, feeding, and changing them. You don't have to talk nonstop from sunup to sundown to hit the target, for example. The data shows that high-talk parents had short five-minute bursts of dynamic conversation more frequently than the rest of us. They had peaks and valleys of talk across the day, meeting or exceeding the forty-turn-per-hour threshold for only about eight of their kids' waking hours. And even within those hours, talk ebbed and flowed noticeably, with just about twenty-five minutes of intensive back-and-forth.

"It's basically five five-minute sessions throughout that hour," explains Jill Gilkerson, the chief research and evaluation officer at LENA. "And during those five minutes, it's just two turns during each minute."

The good news is, you don't have to break out a stopwatch to ensure that you're on track. "Just if you're focused on your child and you can get one turn, try to get one more," Gilkerson advises. "If you've done that, then you've got your two in that minute and that's a great thing. That's going to set you on the road to making this more of a habit, getting the child used to talking, getting you used to talking. And that will just blossom from there."

Plus, you don't have to do this alone. You can enlist the support of friends, family, and other caregivers in your child's life to talk it up with your little one when they can. And, remember, this isn't delivering Shakespearean dialogue. It's just simple back-and-forth with a young child who's still learning to understand and express language. Adorable videos of parents chatting with their babies and toddlers abound on social media and illustrate the ease of turn-taking and extending conversation. In one viral video, comedian and dad DJ Pryor chatted away about the series finale of *Empire,* an admittedly adult show, with his 18-month-old child. Pryor responded to his smiling son's vocalizations as if he understood every babble, and the two exchanged active eye contact, pointing, facial expressions, and gestures that enhanced their communication and connection. Their conversation went like this:

Pryor: *"They need to work on that, right?"*
Kingston: *"Yes."*

Pryor: *"Did you understand it, though?"*

Kingston: *"No" plus indecipherable babble.*

Pryor: *"Oh no, no, not this one. This is the grand finale of this one."*

Kingston: *More babble that sounds like "this one."*

Pryor: *"Yeah, that's the last one."*

Easy enough, right? I like this example of real-world parenting. The dad was slumped over on the couch half watching a favorite television show while giving his little one valuable words and attention. The toddler wasn't watching the show, he was watching Dad, and the show just gave Dad something to talk about. Was this a textbook serve-and-return exchange? No, but it was a darn good one, and judging by the son's smiles, babbles, and gestures, it wasn't the first one. It's so encouraging to see that while the bar *is* high, the recommended level of talk isn't another seemingly impossible standard for busy parents to fall short of. Rather, taking conversational turns in the time you already spend caring for your little one is a powerful practice that can start small in any moment you're together and then build from there. The intention to make your words count and a willingness to use your voice are required. But it's not about spending more time with your child, it's about using the time you already put in a little better.

Pick Your Moments

Most of us don't have access to LENA technology to count the words we exchange with our children and give us personalized feedback reports. Still, we can all benefit from the knowledge that the vast majority of parents could stand to talk a lot more. I asked BJ Fogg, a Stanford University professor and habit expert, how parents might ingrain better conversational routines and patterns in everyday life when we don't have access to cutting-edge monitoring and feedback. He assured me that measurement is "helpful, but not essential."

A count of words or conversational turns can raise parents' awareness of how little they talk to their children, help them understand the gap, and motivate them to make changes. But we don't *need* personalized data to uphold good talk habits. Sticking with a desired behavior over time requires something else, Fogg said—well-chosen reminder prompts to take the specific actions that we're after. As he writes in his book *Tiny Habits,* "No prompt no action."

So, what would a set of habits designed to increase the quality or quantity of talk look like, and what kinds of prompts could trigger them? Good habit options would be anything that encourages us to talk and interact more as described in Chapter 5. And as for the prompts we use to remind us to build those habits, the more specific the trigger, the better. Fogg recommends identifying a particular moment in your daily schedule and formulating a commitment, such as "After I [EVENT], I will [TARGET ACTION]."

Following Fogg's recipe, I came up with the following ideas for prompting more and better parent-child talk. Look them over and see if some would work for you.

GENERAL
- After I hear my baby coo or babble, I will respond in a complete sentence.
- After my child points or gestures, I will look in the direction of interest and describe what I think they pointed to.

MEALTIMES
- After I put breakfast on the table, I will point to and name the foods I'm serving up.
- After we sit down for dinner, I will say a short prayer or expression of gratitude.

DIAPER CHANGES
- After I snap open the baby wipes, I will recite a nursery rhyme.
- After I fasten the diaper, I will point to and describe the clothing I'm about to put on them.

BATHING
- After I turn off the faucet, I will count down out loud: *5-4-3-2-1, bath time!*
- After I lift the baby from the water, I will say, *It's time to dry off!*

NAPTIME OR BEDTIME
- After I swaddle my baby, I will sing a lullaby.
- After I lay the baby in the crib, I will say, *I love you so much.*

IN TRANSIT

- After we walk out the front door, I will ask, *Is it [sunny/ cloudy/rainy] outside today?* Then I'll wait for their response before giving my own answer.
- After I fasten the seat belt, I will say, *We're on our way to [destination].*

STORYTIME

- After I pick up a book, I will describe the cover illustration.
- After I close a book, I will share what I liked most about it.

Importantly, I pegged these habits to some of the most precise, reliable occurrences I could imagine. Not bathing, sleeping, diaper changes, and errand-running in general, but the tiny moments that punctuate long days with littles—turning off the faucet, picking up baby wipes, fastening a seat belt.

Think through the details of your days and identify specific opportunities to initiate conversation, take turns, and ask questions like those just described. Then go a step further and ponder ways to use your environment to support the new habit. For example, you could put a bookmark in your baby's book bin featuring a few questions to ask during a read-aloud or use a changing pad cover with a nursery rhyme toile design to remind you to sing during diaper duty. You'll get to a point where the talking, rhyming, and question-asking are second nature, but nothing beats a good prompt and tangible reminders in the beginning.

Get Tech Support

While anchoring habits to recurring moments in daily life is ideal, I also advocate using technology to keep back-and-forth dialogue top of mind. You can use daycare or preschool texts, emails, or other notifications as prompts to ask your child about their day. Also, try creating your own text, email, or calendar reminders as well, to see what works for you. This could be an automated text at the end of your workday reminding you to share a story or joke with your little one or a pre-dinner notification telling you to put your device away and focus on family while you dine. Don't expect to find the perfect prompt right away. Plan to experiment. If a certain time of day or action feels overwhelming, forgettable, or inconvenient, try a different one.

For example, when I moved to a new house with early-morning trash and recycling collection on Tuesdays, I couldn't for the life of me remember to move our bins out of the shed at the right time. I put it on my digital calendar only to notice it after I was at work. I wrote it on a physical calendar in the kitchen that I never consult. I set up a recurring email reminder, which I also never noticed at an opportune time. Finally, I used an SMS scheduling app to send myself a recurring text message every Tuesday at seven a.m. It worked like a charm, because the text arrived just as I was headed out the door to walk with my daughter to her bus stop. I'd either drag the bins out on the way to the stop or when I walked back afterward.

Once you find a memory aid that works for you, stick with it as long as it works. Don't saddle yourself with judgments like, "I ought to be able to remember this on my own." Be kind to yourself and provide all the support you need. The goal is more back-and-forth talk with kids, not a perfect memory and impeccable habits.

Is a text message or phone alarm the best just-in-time reminder for you? Would a Post-it note on your dashboard be enough to trigger some wordplay in the car, or would it fade into the background and be ignored? Would a stack of TableTopics cards on your kitchen table invite discussion? The prompts each of us needs are as unique as we are, so experiment until you find some that work for you now.

Follow the Child's Lead

Notes to self are great, but your child may just be the ultimate reminder system. Tune in to their speech, from coo to babble to word, and respond in kind—preferably within five seconds—and you'll never have to set an alarm or mark your calendar to get talking.

Araceli Luna Diaz, the former vice president of education for the Concilio, a nonprofit serving Latino families in North Texas that's used LENA devices with families since 2018, says that getting in the habit of "just following what our children are doing and engaging" with is the key. And she's not just spouting program talking points; she's lived it firsthand. When I spoke to her, she was overseeing the initiative—and taking part as a parent participant.

Even though she had long been aware of the benefits of early language, she said her first LENA report showed that her conversational-turns count wasn't even in the 50th percentile. Like so many of us, she'd overestimated how much she talked to her baby.

The LENA Start parent program includes lessons, plus personalized feedback on conversation dynamics and TV/electronic sound in the home, based on the family's talk pedometer recordings. Diaz credits the lessons and reports with sparking aha moments for parents (herself included), where they think, *I can have these conversations with my child, with my baby, and even though they're not speaking, necessarily, they're connecting with me, they're seeing their parents talk to them.*

For example, one LENA Start lesson teaches parents to use mealtimes to build vocabulary and grow kids' brains. There's so much more that parents can say beyond *Here comes the airplane!* as they weave a spoon of mush through the air toward a baby's mouth. LENA encourages parents to talk about the names of food and drinks; categories like fruits, vegetables, and meats; and the utensils and cooking tools they use to prepare and deliver the food. The curriculum also serves up descriptive words to help parents delve into the taste, temperature, texture, colors, size, shape, and quantity of the foods on hand. That's along with action words to describe the biting, chewing, and swallowing that happens at the table, plus phrases like *please* and *thank you* that bring courtesy into play.

Following the child, in this setting, might be noticing them watching you spoon peas onto a plate and saying, *We need more peas on the plate—one, two, three spoonfuls for you!* Or if they turn toward a pan of stir-fry, saying, *Yes, the vegetables are cooking. Do you hear the sizzle? It sounds like* sssss.

Seen this way, most anything a child vocalizes or does can be taken as a nudge to speak with them. Diaz says that when she would see her daughter playing independently, she used that as a reminder to jump in and say, *Hey, what are you playing with? What are these colors?*

With or without a talk pedometer, parents can provide kids with the language nutrition they need and learn to see kids' talk—and even their silent gazing—as calls to conversation.

Limit Kids' Media Use

Sometimes the secret to doing more of one thing is doing less of another. Such is the case with positive, responsive parent-child interactions and kids' media use. If you want to talk more (and more dynamically) with your little one, then limiting the time they (and you) spend glued to a screen is a great place to start.

There was a time when parents had to contend with television only at home, but today smartphones and tablets make media accessible everywhere and at any time. One study, relying on home recordings, found that average daily screen time for 3-year-olds was 172 minutes (2.86 hours) a day, almost triple the maximum of 1 hour per day recommended by the American Academy of Pediatrics and the World Health Organization. And that difference amounts to a significant reduction in talk: 1,139 adult words, 843 child vocalizations, and 194 conversational turns lost per day, to be specific.

Our words and care beat the unresponsive drone of the television or YouTube every time. Unlike older children, toddlers struggle to learn from video—even live video—without someone physically present alongside them to signal that the video content is useful and worth paying attention to. Only we (live, present humans) can provide the specific, tailored responses to kids' utterances that they need to grow vocabulary and understanding.

For kids under 2 years old, the American Academy of Pediatrics guidelines recommend very limited media use, and only when an adult is alongside the child to "co-view, talk, and teach." An example would be when parent and child are video-chatting with out-of-town grandparents. That is, media use for the youngest kids should be brief, interactive, and supervised, in order to benefit little ones. Many parents don't want to hear this, because digital devices have become an integral part of our lives, but the research is clear: showing a baby videos on your phone is not educational.

Indeed, LENA data shows a negative correlation between hours of television and other electronic media detected in recordings and language ability in young children. And a longitudinal study of 2,441 Canadian children found that higher levels of screen time at 24 and 36 months old were associated with worse performance on developmental screenings at 36 and 60 months old, respectively.

Once kids reach preschool age, the time they spend on devices should continue to be in the company of an adult and limited to minutes, not hours, per day. The bright side is, once kids are 3 years old, there is evidence that they can gain valuable alphabetic knowledge from educational media, such as the public television shows *Sesame Street* and *Super Why!*, especially if a parent watches alongside them and discusses and elaborates on the content. So there comes a time when co-viewing video content can create opportunities to talk, build vocabulary, and support kids' development.

And you don't have to commit to watching every episode of *Daniel Tiger* alongside your child to fulfill your parental obligations. A rule of thumb is to watch a few episodes to gauge the quality and appropriateness of a show for your child and model how to engage with its content. Once you've set the tone and shown them how media works, then you can slip away from future episodes to tackle other tasks or take a break.

Preschooler media use is particularly prevalent in households with multiple children because parents use smartphones or tablets to calm or separate bickering siblings. But researchers warn that the quick fix has lasting consequences: "the negative impact brought by excessive screen time will actually increase the burden for parents in later life." That's because each additional hour of screen-time exposure is associated with kids' increased risk for emotional, behavioral, social, and attentional problems down the line.

One strategy that works for many families is drawing hard boundaries around screen use, such as having device-free dinners; setting curfews, after which all devices are docked, charging, and unavailable for use; or creating screen-free rooms or zones at home. Thousands of families have signed on for Screen-Free Saturdays, a nonprofit initiative that promotes unplugging, recharging, and disconnecting from the incessant marketing and manipulations of media and technology companies. You could give it a try and make it an event by powering down devices at sundown on Friday, getting a great night's rest, and fueling a day of family fun and conversation on Saturday.

Put Your Own Phone Down

Parents' own use of media also adversely affects family talk. Numerous studies have found that when parents are on their phones, they're less engaged with and responsive to kids—verbally and nonverbally—sometimes even leading to injury when kids engage in risky bids for attention.

Now, I'm not saying we have to give up fun and games on our phones and devote our full attention to our children every waking second. But let's be honest about where our focus is, what that focus means, and how we might take more opportunities to unplug from devices and tune in to our kids. A survey of 2,000 parents of school-aged children revealed:

- 69 percent of the parents felt "addicted" to their phone

- 62 percent admitted to spending too much time on their cell phone when they were with their kids

- 50 percent had been asked by their child to put their phone away

Knowing better and doing better are two different things. Breaking our bad phone habits often requires serious intervention—mindfulness, that is. Jon Kabat-Zinn has defined mindfulness as "paying attention in a particular way: on purpose, in the present moment, and nonjudgmentally." Practically speaking, mindfulness is the ability to create mental and emotional space between a stimulus and our response. It's cultivating the awareness, self-regulation, and perspective to consciously choose our words and actions (or silence and inaction) in the moment.

In the past decade, numerous studies have investigated mindful parenting and found evidence that it can reduce caregiver stress and coparenting disagreements. Some of the same techniques that have helped parents to snap out of autopilot and respond to kids more skillfully can also serve to help us set aside our phones and converse more in person. Mindfulness-based approaches have helped people battling phone addiction in other contexts. In a pilot study of phone-obsessed university students, mindfulness-based training was associated with a reduction in the students' cravings for their smartphones and in the time they spent using them.

An easy way for parents to curb device use is to make a mindfulness practice out of the phone itself. We can follow the example of writer Marta Brzosko, who "created room for more conscious decision-making" around her phone by taking ten mindful breaths whenever the urge to reach for it emerged.

Similarly, clinical psychologist Mitch Abblett recommends that after we reach for our phones we pause and sit with our devices in hand. Let our thumbs hover over the screen. Take a full, deep breath into the belly and notice whatever thoughts, physical sensations, or emotions arise. Get curious about it all, note whatever feelings come up, and continue to return to attending to the breath.

"We simply (and yet with great difficulty) need to learn to

hold our technology more lightly—with more awareness," Ab-blett explained in a *Mindful* magazine article. "Consider making your phone itself a cue for waking up instead of checking out."

Celebrate Yourself

Now that recording technology has allowed researchers to ana-lyze children's language experience, we can better appreciate parents' pivotal influence. Think of your own child and the im-pact you can make on them over a lifetime, and applaud your-self for what you've read, said, and done already to bolster their literacy. That's all part of a winning early-literacy formula.

Maybe there was a particularly talkative hour this week or a day with less TV than usual—and that's amazing. We don't get better at this by beating ourselves up about our shortcomings. We get better by finding the good, making it regular, and being thoughtful about adding other positive habits to the mix one by one. So focus on what you've done well, rather than wallowing in guilt over any lapses. More carrot, less stick.

Applaud yourself anytime you notice that you've paid loving attention to your child, responded with brain-building lan-guage, sung a nursery rhyme, narrated an activity, turned off the TV, or followed their gaze. Affirmation of the good you've done, when you catch yourself doing it, will do more to cement the habit than dwelling on missteps ever could. It could be a silent fist pump or a whispered *Good job, Mom*. Whatever real-time positive reinforcement resonates with you will wire in the new habit like nothing else.

In fact, Fogg recommends celebrating your habit three times when you're in the early days of forming it—right when you remember to do it, while you're doing it, and immediately after. Bing. Bang. Boom!

"Emotions create habits," he states. "Not repetition. Not frequency. Not fairy dust. Emotions." So go ahead, get in your feelings about any baby steps you take toward becoming a more nurturing, responsive, brain-building caregiver. You deserve it, and your baby does, too.

Try This at Home
Learn to TALK

You now know how critical oral-language experience is for reading development, but making nourishing conversation with babies and young children comes more naturally to some parents than others. So I created the **TALK Method** to help even the quietest parents find something to say while reading or spending time with kids. The next time you're with your child, challenge yourself to:

TAKE TURNS. Even preverbal infants can be dynamic conversational partners, if you let them. Pause to listen for their coos and babbles and to observe their eye movements or facial expressions. When you notice their gaze and utterances, conversation gets much easier because you're responding to their prompts versus initiating talk all on your own. Acknowledge the interests and attention the child shows: *Yes, I hear you.*

I think the dog is pretty silly, too. Your reply fuels early brain development.

ASK QUESTIONS. Want to give babies a language boost, even before they start talking? Try asking questions about a scene unfolding in real life or within the pages of a book you're reading, like *What's that? Do you see the bird?* or just *Ready to turn the page?* A study found that the number of questions moms asked during shared book reading with 10-month-old infants predicted language skills eight months later.

LABEL AND POINT. There's plenty to be said for describing your surroundings or the content of a book page, as well. Labeling (aka naming) objects teaches your child valuable vocabulary. (Note that "labeling" in this context is strictly verbal. It means providing a name or description for something, not placing a printed label onto an object.) Pointing to everyday objects or book illustrations and talking about their colors, shapes, and functions constitute conversation, too. And the finger-to-page or finger-to-object connection helps bring the baby's attention in line with yours. For example, you could say, *There's the umbrella. Right there.* (Pointing.)

KEEP THE CONVERSATION GOING. Look for opportunities to extend, expand, and elaborate on whatever you're talking about. For example, while reading, you could bring book content into the realm of everyday life and experience by linking characters and plot to things the child has experienced. Say something like the following to build on the book without veering too far off topic: *Look! It's raining in the picture. We saw rain outside our window, too.*

Yes, you can have a conversation with an infant who's not yet talking, and you can keep using these same prompts as they age. Taking turns, asking questions, highlighting interesting things, and discussing books never get old. Sooner than you think, your baby will turn into a toddler who points and labels on their own, and then a preschooler who discusses and shares their reactions with you, having learned from your fine example. Trust me, all of this gets easier with time, practice, and attention. One day, more conversation will flow naturally.

JOURNAL PROMPTS

- What are some habits you can establish to support more back-and-forth conversation with your child?

- What daily occurrences (e.g., mealtimes, bath times, naptimes, etc.) and specific moments within them can prompt the habits?

- How can you change your environment to support the habits, such as placing books or talking points in prominent locations at home?

7

Sound Instruction: The Tenor of Reading Success

Everything in writing begins with language. Language begins with listening.

—Jeanette Winterson

In the 1960s, listeners from Los Angeles to London were charmed by Shirley Ellis and her catchy tunes. Archival footage shows her poised in dazzling gowns cinched at the waist just so, the vigor and verve of her vocals holding audiences rapt.

The Congress Records songstress had a single on the Billboard Hot Rhythm and Blues Top 10 list in January 1965, alongside the Temptations' "My Girl," Marvin Gaye's "How Sweet It Is (To Be Loved by You)," the Supremes' "Come See About Me," and Sam Cooke's "A Change Is Gonna Come." Her hit still resounds, although Ellis is too often regarded as an American music history footnote, not a legend like those contemporaries.

The song, inspired by a rhyming game she played as a child, has stayed in rotation through the years in television, movies, commercials, and cover versions. Runway models walked to its rhythms in a Stella McCartney fashion show to rave reviews from *Women's Wear Daily* the same year that a major retailer's commercial featured a family singing it on a road trip. Howard Stern says singing the ditty is his "schtick with kids." Academy Award winner Jessica Lange performed a show-stopping rendition on *American Horror Story* that catapulted the oldie-but-goodie to meme status on TikTok. And the song's title continues to be invoked as a tortured metaphor for trade articles about everything from corporate rebranding efforts to the merits of monogramming.

Yes, "The Name Game" endures. Odds are you know the tune. Something in its rhythm and rules—remove the first consonant of a name; replace it with a B, F, or M; then add a *bo, fo, fee, fi,* or *mo* in the designated spots—keeps the song humming along. Despite prognostications that it was a "novelty tune" destined to disappear when the freshness of its nonsensical humor wore off, it lives on. The inventive wordplay and nods to the hand-clapping, jump-roping culture of black girlhood also won Ellis credit for ushering in a new form of American music. Her picture is *the* image in an encyclopedia entry documenting *proto-rap,* the pre-1980s stylistic forebear to hip-hop's beats, rhymes, and banter. I'd argue that she's also a standard-bearer for another movement that she scarcely could have anticipated—early support for *phonological awareness.*

Let's get down to the nitty-gritty.

Phonological Awareness

Phonological awareness is the conscious ability to recognize and manipulate sound segments within words, and it's right up there with oral language and letter knowledge as a pillar of literacy. It's critical to understand that spoken words can be divided into smaller sounds in order to read in alphabetic writing systems like English. Letters *exist* to represent, in writing, the sequences of sounds that we hear in speech. When kids struggle with reading, an underlying and overlooked cause can be that they have difficulty processing speech sounds. Yet most parents don't think to devote time to bolstering kids' sensitivity to the sounds in words.

To do our part, we parents need to begin paying attention to how words can be sliced and diced into different sound units, such as syllables and less familiar units like—stay with me here—onsets, rimes, and phonemes. Syllables are pronunciation units that include a vowel sound and optional consonant sounds before and/or after the vowel. For example, the word *soccer* has two syllables, and *basketball* has three. An *onset* is the initial consonant or consonant cluster sound in a word—the /t/ sound in *team*, for example, or the /sp/ sound in *spoon*. Some words, like *air,* don't have an onset. The *rime* unit (fraternal twin to *rhyme*), by contrast, is the vowel sound within a syllable plus any consonant sounds that follow the vowel. For example, the "eam" in *team*. *Phonemes* (e.g., /t/, /ē/, or /m/) are the smallest speech-sound units in English—and there are forty-four.

If that sounds like a lot to learn and teach, you can take comfort in a couple of things. One, kids don't need to know all these terms and details. You just need to help them perceive and manipulate the different sounds, which can happen through play. Second, kids' awareness of sounds within words generally develops in a predictable sequence, from larger units like syllables to smaller and smaller ones. And within each size unit, there's a range of ways kids can manipulate the sounds, from rudimentary to complex. Plus, all of this development happens over the course of years, so you've got plenty of time to get up to speed on what skills to nurture now—and next.

In terms of order, children typically recognize that *breakfast* has two syllables before grasping that it starts with a /b/ sound or that it has eight sounds in all—/b/, /r/, /e/, /k/, /f/, /i/, /s/, and /t/. Their ability to blend, segment, and recombine sounds within words also develops with time and experience. Kids can usually compare and contrast words (e.g., notice that *cup* and *pup* rhyme) before they can come up with rhyming words themselves or name the sounds within words. And little ones typically can blend /c/ /u/ /p/ sounds to say *cup* before they can break down *cup* into its three sounds.

Think of these different phonological awareness activities (isolating, blending, segmenting, etc.) at the syllable, onset, rime, and phoneme levels as different presentations of the same fundamental ability. Knowing that these sound analysis skills are all located along a single continuum will help you see how your child is progressing on the road to literacy, according to Jason Anthony, a professor at the University of South Florida who specializes in language and literacy acquisition. In general, children who do well at noticing, pondering, and manipulating sound units within words early on are going to continue to do well and learn to read without difficulty. "The reason it's important to understand that all of these things fall under phonological awareness is that you can actually play with your child, do these sound activities, and encourage their literacy development long before they ever reach formal reading instruction," he explains.

It also means that professionals can identify early which kids are likely to have more difficulty. "We don't have to wait until third grade to decide, 'This child is failing school, he can't read,'" Anthony explains. "Now we're in a much better place to identify a child at risk of reading failure at kindergarten entry or even preschool."

Phonemic Awareness

Of all the skills falling under the phonological awareness umbrella, *phonemic awareness* is the most important for reading. It's the ability to perceive individual sounds, aka phonemes, within spoken words (as opposed to larger units like syllables). I say *perceive* because we hear speech not in a series of discrete sounds but in streams of sounds all influencing their neighbors.

Try this exercise to deepen your understanding. Say the word *sun* aloud. Can you hear exactly where one sound ends and the next begins? No, because there are no audible spaces or separation between the sounds. Furthermore, do you need to pay any attention to the sounds *within* the word to understand its meaning? Not at all. You don't need to break down and separate speech sounds to understand spoken language. You only need to pick apart the sounds within the word because of English's alphabetic system. In order to read the word *sun,* you must perceive three sounds within the sound stream and associate them with the letters S, U, and N. By contrast, in character-based languages like Chinese, attention to these smaller segments of sounds within words isn't required to read.

Kids must spend some time listening for pronunciation (versus for meaning only) to bolster their phonemic awareness skills. And that happens through verbal wordplay *and* through learning about letters' names and sounds, both of which parents can facilitate. You could prompt your child to compare different starting sounds in rhyming words like *sun* versus *bun.* You could play around with tongue twisters that emphasize specific sounds, like *Sandra's silly sunglasses shone sharply in the sun.* The contrasts among similar words and the repetition of the same sound across different words both help nurture phoneme awareness. It also helps greatly to talk about the sounds letters make while referencing the letters in writing, too. Similarly, looking at words while analyzing their sound structure gives little ones a concrete way to think about speech sounds.

Kids who can notice, blend, and segment phonemes are well on their way to recognizing words, to reading, and to spelling. And you should be intentional about helping your child get there, urges Gail Gillon, director of the University of Canterbury Child Well-Being Research Institute. "Lots of rhyming stories are a great introduction," she says. "But you need to move to getting even young children to really tune into the first sounds as the starting point."

How to Nurture Phonological Awareness

A great deal of what we associate with learning is informed by what we experienced in our own schools. But teaching needn't look like a formal classroom with a parent at a whiteboard and the child behind a desk (or computer). Family teaching at home and on the go should be much more organic than that, and when it comes to phonological awareness, at least, it can definitely be fun and on the fly.

It's not drill and kill. It's singing "The Name Game." It's talking in pig Latin. It's playing I Spy with beginning sounds or rhyming words instead of colors. (*I spy something that rhymes with* tike. *Yes, the bike!*)

When you recite nursery rhymes, you're heightening kids' sensitivity to the syllables and the beginning, middle, and ending sounds within words. The stress patterns of classics like "Jack and Jill Went up the Hill" help them learn about syllables and rhymes, important phonological awareness skills. And the alliteration in *Peter Piper picked a peck of pickled peppers* accentuates the /p/ sound and distinguishes it from surrounding sounds, a finer-grained level of phoneme sensitivity.

You can easily build phonological awareness anytime, anywhere, with just your voice and your child's attention. You don't need books (although they can help). You don't need paper. You don't need a table. You don't even need to be still—neighborhood strolls or car, bus, or subway rides present lovely opportunities for this kind of banter. Just keep in mind your child's age and find a few go-to activities to incorporate into the things you're already doing together. Here are some ideas to get you started.

Focus on syllable-blending (*bat* plus *man* equals *batman*) and syllable-clapping activities with 2- and 3-year-olds.

- How many syllables are in *elevator*? **Four**
- Put this word together: *cup* plus *cake*. **Cupcake**
- Say the syllables in *elephant*. **El-e-phant**
- What's the word *applesauce* without *apple*? **Sauce**

For 3- and 4-year-olds, emphasize rhyming skills, along with blending and segmenting onsets and rhymes.

- Do *cup* and *pup* rhyme? **Yes**. Do *cup* and *cake* rhyme? **No**
- Tell me some words that rhyme with *win*. **Bin, kin, sin, thin**
- Put this word together: C-at. **Cat**
- Divide *sleep* into two parts. **Sl-eep**

With 4-year-olds, dig into individual sounds as your child gets more familiar with the alphabet.

- Which words start with the same sound: *bug, bowl, fish*? **Bug, bowl**
- What's the first sound in *zoo*? **/z/**
- What sound is the same in *cow, cat, camel, kangaroo*, and *koala*? **/k/**

By ages 5 and 6, kids may initiate sound games on their own, by doing things like talking in pig Latin to friends. *Ooday ouyay ememberray atthay amegay?*

- Which word starts with a different sound—*bad, bat, rag, bag*? **Rag**
- Put this word together: /y/ /e/ /s/. **Yes!**
- What sounds do you hear in the word *bat*? **/b/ /a/ /t/**
- What word do you get if you add /b/ to /r/ /a/ /g/? **Brag**
- The word is *bug*. Change the /b/ to /h/. What's the new word? **Hug**

Next, typically after 6 years old, kids can get adept at blending, segmenting, deleting, adding, and substituting sounds in words. That's when you can add phonological play like spoonerisms into the mix. These are when you swap the starting sounds of two words (usually to comical effect). Sometimes they occur naturally in conversation when you accidentally say things like "I zipped the skoom meeting" instead of "I skipped the Zoom meeting." But you can intentionally mix up initial sounds as a game, and get your little one in on the action. Just explain the game and give examples, like: *Let's mix up some sounds. Instead of saying, "It's dinnertime," we can say, "It's tinner dime," if we flip-flop the starting sounds. What happens if you swap the starting sounds in "Tootsie Roll"? Yes, that would be "rootsie toll"!*

This is all meant to be wordplay, not an interrogation! Get excited and cheer together when your child solves the puzzle. If they struggle or don't get it, laugh together. A great irony of raising readers is that the critically important, life-trajectory-altering, high-stakes work of building these foundational skills is best done with the lightest, nearly imperceptible touch. The subtler the accumulation of moments of speech, song, and play over the course of years, the better, experts agree.

As you nurture these skills, remember to keep things light, fun, and encouraging. "If you're trying to do exercise and it's really tough and you've got a trainer or someone telling you you're not getting it right, you just stop going," Gillon from the University of Canterbury says. "And it's the same with children. They like to do things that they're getting lots of positive praise and encouragement for. If it's fun, they'll keep doing it."

Or, put another way, *if it's not fun, don't do it.*

Home Language Advantage

Parents who speak languages other than English at home may worry about whether they are pronouncing English words correctly, and they can be hesitant to work on phonological awareness as a result. Don't even worry about it. There's evidence to suggest that phonological awareness originally developed in a different language—like the parent and child's first language—transfers to phonological awareness and improves word-reading skills in English. All languages have underlying sound structures that children need to gain familiarity with, so there's value in working on phonological awareness in whatever language the parent or caregiver is most comfortable with. Take pride in your first language, keep it central to your child's life, and seize opportunities for wordplay. You can make up silly sentences with words beginning with the same sound in another language just as easily as in English.

"Particularly for parents of young children that might be struggling themselves with learning a language or English might not be their first language, they worry sometimes, 'Should I be just trying to speak English?'" Gillon explains. "I'm saying the opposite: No. Use your own language that you're confident in when they're little, and get them to hear the sounds in your home language and develop those skills, because that's an absolute treasure."

There's beauty and consequence in using your own language, she says. "It's important for little ones that they just start hearing the sounds in their language—being consciously aware of the first sounds and words, listening for the rhythm of their language, and really bringing their attention to the sound structure of their language."

Early on, kids are developing the cognitive ability to hear sounds in words, starting with listening to the rhythms of songs and everyday language. So even if it's a goal for your child to learn English, in this early stage there's a benefit to using your home language to build phonological skill.

Indeed, there's evidence for cross-language transfer of phonological skills. "It's not necessarily a direct transfer for all languages, because it does depend on the different languages you are learning, but it's certainly helpful," Gillon adds. "If you're good at phonological awareness in your first language, you will pick up those same types of phonological awareness skills when you come to learn a second language. And equally, if you struggle in one language, you will struggle in another."

But don't stop there. If English fluency is your goal, seek out opportunities for your child to gain exposure to written and spoken English, too. The research is still accumulating, but there's an emerging case that phonological awareness in a second language is heavily influenced by oral-language ability in that language and how different the first and second languages are from each other. The stronger a child's overall language experience in both, the better.

And remember: You yourself don't have to provide all the language experience your child needs. You can give them the best of what you have and seek out what you can't directly provide. Sometimes friends or family members who speak the target language may be just the conversation partners, word-game players, and nursery-rhyme singers your child needs. Sometimes you may find them at library programs or in early-childcare centers. Audiobooks, recorded music, and cartoons in the second language provide language exposure, too (albeit without the total benefits of a live human providing personal responses). Get clear on what you can give and get intentional about supplementing the rest.

Accentuate the Differences

Even native English-speaking parents worry that their regional, cultural, or ethnic accents or dialect may hinder their ability to teach a child the sounds of "standard" English. These are complex, weighty issues. Sometimes racially and linguistically marginalized kids grow up to be teachers who question their own grasp of the language.

Marcelle Haddix, dean of the School of Education at the University of Wisconsin–Madison, had a student once ask, "How can I teach reading when I can't even pronounce the words right?" If a college student preparing to make a profession of teaching carried this level of doubt, many more parents—untrained and unsupported—must feel even more hesitant.

Some dialects are more closely aligned with the English taught in school. Others—even those that are just as complex, long-standing, rule-governed, and legitimate—are wrongly dismissed and thought to be a degraded version of "the standard." But every single speaker of English learns a dialect (a particular combination of grammar, vocabulary, and pronunciation), and none guarantees literacy acquisition.

In fact, respect for and exploration of dialect variations can be wonderful launching pads for language and literacy learning. "Sensitivity to dialectical differences can be taught and can be learned," Jason Anthony says. "And there's some research that shows that individuals who can code-switch fluently may actually be at a metalinguistic advantage." Translation: People who can move between dialects or variations with ease may have a better awareness of language that boosts linguistic processing and learning. The trick is to embrace and get curious about the differences between dialects, versus minimizing or ignoring them. Do your best to describe the sounds and syllables as you hear them, and point out how others might say or hear them differently.

For example, final /d/ consonants are often not pronounced in African American Vernacular English (AAVE), a dialect that originated hundreds of years ago and is spoken by the majority of black elementary schoolers in the United States. That little omission of vibration of the vocal cords means that many speakers of that dialect often initially spell unconventionally—for

example, writing *salat* for *salad*. Of course, all kids spell unconventionally at first for various reasons, driven by their personal
oral-language experience and knowledge of English writing.
This is no different than the pronunciation variations that lead
British kids to hear and spell *ticket* as *tickit* at higher rates than
Australian kids who pronounce the second vowel sound differently.

This is nothing to be ashamed of or shy away from. Instead,
observe and embrace the differences. Talk about them, bring
attention to them, and in doing so deepen your child's language
experience and pride in cultural and linguistic roots. The greater
risk is depriving your little one of valuable learning opportunities because you're afraid of getting it wrong. As Anthony puts
it, "It's more about just giving practice and exposure than it is
being technically precise."

Kids leap into reading from a foundation of oral language, letter
knowledge, and phonemic awareness. In an alphabetic writing
system like ours, you can't read without being able to identify
individual sounds and associate those sounds with the letters
that represent them. This is why there's a handbook of linguistics that devotes most of a section to "The Name Game." It's also
why educators looking to gauge preschoolers' readiness to read
may teach them the song—it helps them check the kids' ability
to manipulate the sounds within words.

And so a game from Shirley Ellis's childhood that likely
helped her hone her own reading skills is immortalized in mu-

sic, pop culture, and early literacy. Even if she's no longer a household name, her influence is undeniable.

Try This at Home
Add Sights to Sounds

Phonological awareness is a critical pillar of early literacy that parents don't hear enough about and could do a lot to nurture (in easy, fun, free ways). This chapter described several activities—from "The Name Game" and spoonerisms to pig Latin and nursery rhymes—that you can use to raise your child's awareness of the sounds within words.

One pro tip for taking your efforts to the next level is to get physical by bringing objects and gestures into sound lessons. There's something about a strong visual or tactile element in addition to the auditory dimension that helps kids grasp the tasks at hand.

When highlighting syllables or onsets and rimes, you can put your hands in fists to illustrate different segments and bring them together to show blends. *What does putting* cup *[hold up one fist] and* cake *[hold up the other fist] together make?* Cupcake *[bring fists together].* The same goes for segmenting the /k/ sound from the "at" in *cat.*

You have only two hands, so you'll need some other tools when tackling multisyllabic words or when you want to address more individual sounds in words. Blocks, coins, or other small tokens that you already have can make sound tasks more concrete—and interesting.

For example, you could line up four pennies to represent the different sounds in the word *sled*: /s/, /l/, /e/, /d/. You could say each sound slowly while pointing at the coin that represents it and then run your finger across each coin quickly as you pronounce the whole word. The physical materials help bring attention to the individual sounds. Later you can replace the objects with letters, in the form of magnetic letters or alphabet blocks or simply letters written on paper.

JOURNAL PROMPTS

- What did you learn in this chapter about how the sounds within words relate to kids' reading development?

- What level of phonological awareness should you focus on with your child now—syllables, rhymes, initial sounds, ending sounds, phonemes?

- What will your go-to rhymes, games, or activities be?

- What are good times in your day to work on phonological awareness?

8

L Is for Liberation: How to Help Kids Crack the Alphabetic Code

The alphabet is an abolitionist. If you would keep a people enslaved, refuse to teach them to read.

—*Harper's Weekly* editorial, 1867

Do you know what it takes to possess a letter? To unravel the mystery of two-dimensional scrawls on a page? To know a lowercase l from an uppercase I from a numeral 1 from a line? To recognize an L in uppercase and lowercase, in cursive and print, in Times New Roman and Comic Sans alike?

It's a gargantuan climb for your child to learn these secrets—the letter names, their shapes, their sounds, their nature, their functions, and how they work together. Taking possession of the twenty-six letters of our alphabet is a victory, a claim to freedom and to power. Though most of us can't recall exactly how we came to know the letters intimately and automatically, the stories of those who do remember are instructive.

Take famed abolitionist Frederick Douglass. His road to reading started out forthrightly enough, when his enslaver's wife taught him the alphabet and a few simple words. But this early instruction was cruelly cut short by a lesson his teacher received: that literacy and slavery were incompatible. In an autobiography, Douglass recalls his enslaver warning her that an enslaved person "should know nothing but to obey his master—to do as he is told to do . . . Now, if you teach [Douglass] how to read, there would be no keeping him. It would forever unfit him to be a slave."

Mass literacy was so threatening to enslavers that they routinely met black people's attempts at reading with whippings, amputations, and murder. Cutting the finger of the offending reader down to the first joint was common. Mississippi law made corporal punishment "not exceeding thirty-nine lashes" the price to be paid by groups of black people—enslaved or free—who dared assemble to learn reading or writing. South Carolina created stiffer and stiffer anti-literacy statutes between 1740 and 1834, eventually punishing black readers with up to fifty lashes. And even in states like Maryland where the law didn't prohibit such teaching, custom often did.

Historian Heather Andrea Williams explains how denying literacy was meant to deny enslaved people's very humanity and prolong their captivity. "Reading indicated to the world that this so-called property had a mind, and writing foretold the ability to construct an alternative narrative about bondage itself," she writes. "Literacy among slaves would expose slavery, and masters knew it."

And so Douglass heard his enslaver's tirade for what it

was—a clear admission that literacy was no less than "the pathway from slavery to freedom." Thus motivated, he set out to learn to read "with high hope, and a fixed purpose, at whatever cost of trouble."

He mastered the letters S, L, F, and A from the scribblings of Baltimore shipyard carpenters who marked timber placements *starboard* or *larboard* side and *forward* or *aft*. He plied poor Irish immigrant boys with bread to get them to teach him the letters they knew. Then Douglass snuck away to scrawl the treasured letters with a lump of chalk on a board fence, brick wall, or pavement, and copied them in the spaces left in a white child's old *Webster's Spelling Book* until he knew them cold.

Literacy, starting with the recognition and naming of twenty-six letters, offered enslaved people a measure of mobility, privacy, and liberty that was as precious as life itself. Thousands of enslaved men, women, and children ventured on this dangerous, covert pursuit of the alphabet and the powerful words it made by any means they could, and an estimated 5 percent succeeded in learning to read by 1860.

Perhaps thousands more perished trying.

Your child's journey won't be this perilous. But make no mistake, literacy today is no less powerful a means of resistance and liberation. And there are still considerable obstacles to its attainment, especially for children who are poor, brown, or black.

Letters are the building blocks of the written words that kids must learn to read, and in most U.S. schools, letter *names* are the very "language of instruction." But there's marked disparity in letter-name knowledge, a foundational skill that is incredibly influential in their academic trajectories, as children approach kindergarten. Lower-socioeconomic-status students tend to know substantially fewer letter names in preschool than higher-socioeconomic-status kids, which sets them up to struggle with reading and spelling down the line.

Sit in on a typical kindergarten class and at some point you're likely to hear dialogue such as:

- "How do you spell *cat*? **C-A-T.**"
- "What's the first letter of *apple*? **A!**"
- "What letter makes the /m/ sound? **That's right, M makes the /m/ sound.**"

To make sense of these questions, students need to both know the letter names and have a sense of the function that letters serve in words. Otherwise, children can't engage in the crucial conversations about reading and writing that they are meant to learn from.

Letter names give children the labels they need to connect the different manifestations of a letter in their memory—uppercase or lowercase, print or cursive, one font or another. And because many letter names bear some resemblance to their letter sounds (B says /b/, for example), little ones who have learned letter names have a tool for grasping and remembering the sounds they must learn in order to read. In fact, alphabetic knowledge is among the most robust, reliable early predictors of future reading success—and failure—that we have. It has long been established that assessments of kids' letter-name knowledge in kindergarten do a better job of foretelling later reading achievement than a number of other linguistic, memory, and learning measures.

Letter-name knowledge is so critical that it's become a major target of early education in the United States. Preschool, kindergarten, and early intervention program curricula often emphasize it, and kindergarten readiness tests assess it. And yet even the best classroom efforts offer too little too late for far too many children.

Heartbreaking research found that children from lower socioeconomic backgrounds who enrolled in a preschool program knew significantly fewer letter names at the start—and end—of preschool than their higher-socioeconomic-background peers. The two groups of children in the program, which had been rated "high quality" by the state of Ohio, showed about the same rate of growth in letter-name knowledge during their time with it. But the children from lower socioeconomic backgrounds couldn't catch up to their peers, so the gap remained at the end of the year. The program wasn't *high enough* quality in this respect to ensure that all of the students entered kindergarten poised to thrive.

One large-scale pre-K evaluation showed that kids who had attended a high-quality preschool for an entire year recognized, on average, nine more letters than kids who had just begun preschool. Unless your child enrolls in preschool with ten uppercase letters already under their belt, or continues learning letters at home, that pace of learning isn't going to get the job done.

It's a challenge for teachers to devote enough time to assessing which uppercase and lowercase letters particular children don't know and then teaching those specific letters. Amid all the lessons in social skills, imaginative play, shapes, numbers, and colors, this crucial instruction gets curtailed.

As a parent, you must set your own letter-name knowledge standards, and you must set them high. Do not take your child's possession of the twenty-six letters of the alphabet for granted. Research suggests that preschoolers who can name eighteen uppercase letters and fifteen lowercase letters are well on their way to reading, and those who can't are likely to struggle. Aim for your child to know every letter name—uppercase and lowercase—by sight by the end of kindergarten, in line with many states' standards.

And there's no doubt that you can help. Teaching twenty-six letters is well within even the busiest parents' capacity, especially if you start as soon as your child is old enough to recognize them, around 3 years old. Just point out letters, state their names and sounds, and describe their distinctive visual features—no extensive planning or elaborate lessons required, just light touches and incidental teaching in everyday life with your child.

There are countless opportunities to point out letters in the books you read or on the signs and labels you come across in your daily activities. You can pause on a neighborhood walk, gesture toward a stop sign, and say: *Look at the stop sign. S-T-O-P spells* stop. *Do you see the letter S? It curves this way and that.* (Trace an S shape in the air.) You can also whip out a sheet of paper in an idle moment, write a letter on it (say, your child's first initial or your own), and start a discussion about its features.

Some parents may object to the goal of knowing all the letters by the end of kindergarten, on the grounds that they learned their letters later in life and they read fine. The problem with that thinking is that, rightly or wrongly, U.S. elementary school standards are much higher today. Educators' expectations spiked after the signing of the No Child Left Behind Act in 2002 and the expansion of early-childhood education programs. Public school kindergarten teachers in 2010 were more than twice as likely to "strongly agree" or "agree" that kids should learn to read in kindergarten and that parents should ensure that their kids know the alphabet prior to entry, compared with their colleagues in 1998. These raised expectations were, in many instances, even "more pronounced among schools serving high percentages of low-income and non-White children." Children who don't know their letters in kindergarten are likely to struggle with classroom instruction, fall further behind peers, and experience feelings of anxiety and inadequacy.

You may worry that aspiring to these standards may be pushing kids too far too fast. There are educational traditions of high literacy achievement that don't even commence reading instruction until kids are 7 years old—such as in Waldorf schools or in Finland's public school system. But starting formal reading instruction that late makes sense only within an educational framework expressly designed to support it, which is absolutely not the case in U.S. public schools.

The main reason to build alphabetic knowledge before kindergarten isn't that it's impossible for kids to learn it later, but that our current system offers insufficient support. Most of our public schools simply are not equipped to meet kids where they are. They are set up to teach particular content at particular grade levels, and if your child isn't there—good luck. Moreover, as children advance through the grades, their access to foundational reading instruction and effective intervention declines.

Simply put, parents need to prepare their children to thrive in the system we *have*. If your child is going to be traditionally schooled in the United States, be ready to navigate the customs, curriculum, and expectations found there. The good news is that any caregiver with even basic literacy, few to no materials, and just minutes a day can get them ready—with the right knowledge and approach.

Young children are completely capable of building alphabetic knowledge prior to school. And doing so with a parent, through play, games, and incidental teaching, is an effective—and enjoyable—route. If you haven't worked on alphabetic knowledge with your child, or you sense that they are "behind," according to today's standards, don't panic. Knowledge is power, and now that you're aware of what your child needs to learn, you can start where they are and help them climb.

Teaching Letter Names the Smart Way

As readers ourselves, parents often fail to grasp what a leap it is even to see letters as distinct from other images and graphics in print. To know an O from a circle or an H from a stick figure is the result of a long learning process, a slow-growing awareness of print and its properties. At first, pictures, letters, and numbers are all a bunch of 2D marks to be deciphered.

Parents with savvy and resources, though, tend to use a wide range of activities and contexts at home to build and reinforce alphabetic skills. They play with magnetic letters, point out letters on household items, read alphabet books, and talk about the letters in their child's name. In questionnaires, in-the-know parents reported using an average of *fourteen* out of eighteen different home-teaching contexts, from storybooks and shopping lists to letter blocks and flash cards, to engage kids with the alphabet. Brief teachable moments pave the way.

Unsurprisingly, the parents who reported teaching the ABCs the most frequently tended to be those with high expectations of what their kids should know before first grade. These parents had wisely linked the letter work they did with future school achievement. And you can do the same.

What you say to your child about letter shapes, names, and sounds—and when—matters. When you take responsibility for teaching your child the alphabet before they start kindergarten, you're doing crucial work to support their later success. Speak with knowledge and intention, seize everyday moments, and structure your home and schedule to support deliberate learning. Here are a few ideas to get you started:

CALL LETTERS BY THEIR NAMES. While some people prefer to teach letter sounds before letter names, the fact of the matter is that kids need to know both—and instruction is simpler for parents when you have unique and consistent labels. I say teach letter names and sounds at the same time. "Clearly, it is easier to say, 'Point to the A,' than to say, 'Point to the letter that says /æ/ (or /ä/ or /ā/ or /uh/),'" pioneering researcher Marilyn Jager Adams explains.

Think of the names as labeled buckets in which kids collect all their encounters with a letter—uppercase, lowercase, print, cursive, its various sounds, and so on. Over time and through exposure, in one's memory, "the label provides a means of bonding together all of one's experiences with a to-be-learned concept," Adams writes. "In doing so, it can only hasten the recognition of the similarities of the concept across its occurrences."

Recent research continues to provide support for using letter names. Studies suggest that letter-name knowledge benefits young children's spelling, for example—a crucial component of literacy development. And researchers have found evidence that combining letter-name training with letter-sound instruction accelerates letter-sound learning.

Parents' talk about letters and use of letter names can start at any time but becomes particularly powerful when kids are 3 years old and can focus on letters in print. At that point, they can begin to forge letter identities through repeated experience with their shapes, names, and sounds. This is a good time to start pointing out letters that are prominent in your home or neighborhood, such as on a stop sign, monogrammed item, or cereal box. Remember to play I Spy: *I spy with my little eye the letter S. It curves around like this.* (Draw an S shape in the air.) *Do you see an S?*

ASSESS LETTER-NAME KNOWLEDGE. Take care to determine which, if any, letters your child already knows. You may be surprised by the knowledge they already possess.

You can find out by writing uppercase and lowercase letters on separate index cards, showing them to your child in a random order, and asking them to name them. Be sure to record the date and whether they responded correctly or not. If the response surprises you or is noteworthy in some respect, jot that down on the back of the card as well. These casual notes about what your child knows, and when, will prove invaluable as their journey advances. This kind of assessment is the basic method that literacy researchers use to see which letters kids know.

If index cards feel too clinical for you, check letter-name knowledge using whatever materials or circumstances feel fun to you and your child. You can write letters anywhere—in sand at the beach, on a plate with syrup, in shaving cream on the side of the bathtub. The important thing is to take note of your child's response to the question *What letter is this?*

DRAW ATTENTION TO LETTERS AND THEIR SHAPES. Remember that the distinctions between a letter, a number, and other writing and drawings are not immediately apparent to young children. These are things that they learn slowly and through repeated attention, experience, and explanation.

Start the process by pointing out the differences among the symbols you see in storybooks and daily life. Bring your child's attention to letters wherever you encounter them. Point to them, trace them, and have your child do the same, so you know they are locked in on these particular symbols.

Analyses of parent-child conversations have found salient differences in the *content* of parents' alphabet talk. When you encounter a letter in a book, on a sign, or elsewhere in the world, you could talk about it in many ways. Describe its size, color, or shape, for example. Any description could build helpful knowledge and vocabulary, but *only one* of those characteristics—the shape—speaks directly to the letter's essential visual identity and builds the early-literacy foundation we're after.

When kids first start to focus on letter shapes at around 3 years old, many letters look alike to them. Both lowercase p and lowercase q are circles with lines attached, and differentiating left from right can take time. Same for lowercase b and d.

To help your child notice differences among letters, make a point of talking about the curves, lines, hooks, humps, and dots, as well as the breaks and junctures within them. Those five descriptive words provide the main vocabulary you need to consistently and helpfully describe letters for your child. For example, you can highlight things like where the curve begins and ends in a C or where the lines intersect in an X. You can compare how there is one hump in the lowercase letter n and two in lowercase m; trace the long hook in an uppercase J; point out the dots in i and j; and so on. Visit readingforourlives.com/letters to download printable resources for letter teaching.

Letter Parts

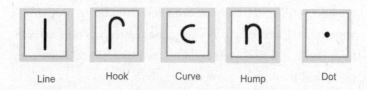

| Line | Hook | Curve | Hump | Dot |

SING, THEN SAY, THE ABCS. Many parents' alphabet-teaching efforts begin and end with "The Alphabet Song." While it's fun to sing it in the car or around the house, usually there's no reference made to print while doing it, so kids aren't making the connection between the lyrics and the individual letters that make up the song. Moreover, in the song, the letters are all blurred together, leaving L-M-N-O-P sounding more like *ella-minnowpee*. Singing the song is great for building another skill—learning alphabetic order—and giving kids an introduction to letter names. But to help kids connect all the dots sooner, try sometimes saying the song, versus only singing it, and pointing to each letter as you articulate it. Visit readingforourlives .com/letterchart to download a cute alphabet chart that's perfect for this activity.

ENCOURAGE YOUR CHILD TO MAKE LETTERS HOWEVER THEY CAN. Letter talk also spurs kids' experiments with forming the letters themselves—whether by writing them or making the shapes out of Play-Doh or Popsicle sticks. And that tactile experience with letters, in turn, creates even more opportunities for kids to ponder and engage with letters' distinctive features. A virtuous circle!

There are countless variations and activities for teaching letters. Kids can trace letters, draw them in Jell-O, make them out of macaroni, or build them from sticks. The important thing to remember (before you fall down the rabbit hole of letter activities on Pinterest) is that the lesson is in your voice and your description of the letters' form and function. If you're not talking about the letters' lines, curves, names, and sounds, your child isn't getting what they need.

TEACH UNKNOWN LETTERS FROM EASIEST TO HARDEST. Many classrooms take a letter-a-week approach and march through the alphabet from A to Z. Don't follow that example. Kids vary greatly in which letters they know when, and your approach should reflect their individuality. Spend more time and energy on the letters your child doesn't know, and teach the unknown letters from easiest to hardest.

All kids pick up some letters more easily than others, based on factors that include the distinctiveness of their shape, their order in the alphabet, and how frequently they appear in print. Studies have found evidence that the first initial of the child's name and the letters O, B, and A are among the easiest to name and write.

Often, we parents make a big deal out of our children's names, showing the child their name in print, teaching them to write it, or labeling and monogramming belongings with it. Many learn the name of their initial first because of the special attention parents have given that letter and its personal relevance. In fact, one study found that kids whose parents had emphasized their first initial at 3 and 4 years old tended to be stronger readers at the end of kindergarten.

Except for a kid's own first initial, O is usually among the first letters learned, because of its distinctive circular shape and the similarity of its uppercase and lowercase versions. Research suggests that kids tend to learn U and V last. These trends have been documented across a wide array of early-childhood programs, including Head Start, public pre-kindergarten, and private childcare settings.

There's no definitive sequence, but researchers have called the following a "typical order" for letter-name acquisition. It may be useful to refer to this order in teaching your own child—but again, responding to their interests and knowledge is most important.

EARLIEST	LETTER NAMES
	Your Child's First Initial
	O
	B
	A
	C
	X
	PSEHT
	WMRKD
	FLYZ
	GJNIQ
	U
LATEST	V

And there's no strong evidence to support teaching only one letter a week, as many teachers do. In fact, a faster pace of letter instruction seems especially beneficial for the lowest-performing children.

Help Off the Shelf

Literacy skill work gets a bad rap. Teachers and parents decry the early onset of "drill and kill," but there are many ways to deepen understanding of letter shapes, names, sounds, and functions without resorting to long lectures or intense practice. In fact, it's best to just get in the habit of pointing out letters briefly and repeatedly through the course of everyday life. You can remind yourself to talk about letters by keeping physical prompts at hand, like alphabet books, puzzles, and wall charts.

Alphabet puzzles give kids a feel for the look and shape of letters. Go for the large, 3D letter-block variety that fits the letter shapes into predefined slots on a puzzle board, versus a flat jigsaw.

When the puzzle pieces are letter-shaped, whether uppercase or lowercase, they draw kids' attention to the lines, curves, and angles of letters, and tucking the letters into the appropriate slots requires getting the left/right and top/bottom orientation correct, too. A number of vendors make personalized name puzzles, so kids can play with letters of individual significance. The pieces should be large enough that a toddler can grasp and place them with ease.

Alphabet books can prompt valuable thought and discussion about letters—if you choose them wisely, read them thoughtfully, and explain them intentionally. The "A is for . . ." format is so familiar to parents that we can overlook its complexity. Even the most basic ABC book requires extensive background knowledge and language to understand. Researchers estimate that kids pick up, on average, fewer than three new letters after four readings of an alphabet book. So again, the point is that we've got to stay at it over time and seize a variety of opportunities to make letter lessons stick.

In the beginning, it's not the print on the page alone, but parents' pauses, pointing, and conversation that allow kids' alphabetic knowledge to grow. Your talk while reading an alphabet book might be saying things like *This page says "A is for Apple." This is the letter A.* (Point to A.) *A makes the /a/ sound. Can you say /a/? Can you hear that* apple *starts with /a/? A-P-P-L-E spells* apple. (Point to each letter.)

The signs, product labels, and logos that we encounter in everyday life (aka *environmental print*) also make impactful teaching tools. Many parents naturally point to words and read them aloud at home, during play, and while out and about in their communities. But far fewer bring their children's attention to the level of individual letters embedded in the signs and labels.

Researchers found evidence that a program that coached middle-socioeconomic-status parents in how to focus their 2- to 5-year-olds' attention on specific letters led to significant improvement in letter knowledge and reading ability. The program trained parents to use multisensory strategies, including pointing (visual), saying (auditory), moving (kinesthetic), and tracing (tactile). Importantly, the program taught parents to use directional language (the terms *up*, *down*, *around*, and *across*) to describe how the letters are formed, which helps kids notice and recall their distinctive features.

All parents should have environmental print strategies in their toolkits, but it's especially useful for those who lack access to children's books at home. The signs around your neighborhood and the labels on your clothes and home products have everything you need to support your young child's emergent literacy. If you're folding laundry, for example, pull out a graphic tee or a shirt with a logo, trace a letter, talk about it and ask your child to do the same. I counted twenty-two different letters on a Trader Joe's paper grocery bag alone. Between the store name, website address, instructions to hold both handles, call to reuse and recycle, and illustration of Cidre Mousseux, we had the alphabet minus K, Q, V, and Z. That's fodder for many rounds of letter I Spy.

Ibi Zoboi, a Haitian American author of young adult fiction, once spoke powerfully about this during a panel at the Texas Book Festival. Zoboi said she grew up in an environment where there were "absolutely no bookstores around," but she was not without rich stories and language exposure. She said that her love of speculative fiction grew from the political tales often embellished with magical realism that her mom, aunt, and other relatives told about their home country. And she gleaned volumes from their words and the everyday language around her home.

"I'm a child of the '80s and I watched a lot of TV," she explains. "When people asked me what were the books that I loved growing up, I cannot always say, but I don't want anybody to look down on me or any children like myself who did not have books in the home. We had TV and that's also a form of storytelling. We had the back of cereal boxes. Magazines."

Work with what you've got to give your kids the lessons that they need most. Unlike classroom teachers who have limited time, myriad goals, and kids of varying abilities and prior knowledge, parents have the benefit of a limited number of children and years of everyday interactions. For the most part, your success will boil down to time and consistency. Don't worry about making mistakes. There's no perfect instruction. Just get talking, so your child can get learning.

Try This at Home
Give Letters Shape

The importance of diving into letter names, sounds, and shapes when kids are as young as 3 cannot be overstated. Preschoolers are fully capable of learning these building blocks of reading. And you can make it fun and gradual by introducing letters lightly over time in everyday life through books, signage, labels, monograms, toys, and other print.

Easy does it, and emphasizing the letter shapes is the way to go for parents. Any time you spend describing letters' curves and lines brings your child's attention to defining features, helps them distinguish among letters, and supports writing. Plus, this talk also often naturally segues into discussing letter names and sounds. For example, if you are teaching a child to spell their name you might say things like the following:

T-O-M spells *Tom*.

This is the letter T. T says /t/. It's made of one short line and one long line. It goes this way to the right and this way down. (Write the letter.) Can you say /t/? Can you write a T?

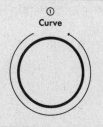

This is the letter O. It is a big circle. You write it by starting here and making a curve all the way around. (Write the letter.) O says /o/. Can you say /o/?

This is the letter M. It's made of two long lines and two short lines. A long line goes down this way. A short line goes slanted here and another short line slants this way. A long line goes down here. (Trace the lines.) M says /m/. Can you say /m/?

JOURNAL PROMPTS

- What does your child know about letters? Can they tell a letter apart from drawings or numbers?

- Which uppercase and lowercase letters can your child name if they see them?

- What print do you have in your home and neighborhood that you can call attention to (e.g., magnetic letters, monogrammed items, books, and magazines)? Where could you add more print to your home, such as framed letter art or favorite quotes?

- When writing or scribbling on their own, does your child use letters at all? If so, which letters do they write? Does their writing reflect the knowledge that letters represent sounds?

9

Word Wisdom: How to Spell Your Way to Better Reading

For, though the origin of most of our words is forgotten, each word was at first a stroke of genius, and obtained currency, because for the moment it symbolized the world to the first speaker and to the hearer. The etymologist finds the deadest word to have been once a brilliant picture.

—Ralph Waldo Emerson

I hail from Akron, Ohio, a city most famous (depending on who you ask) for being the former rubber capital of the world, the birthplace of LeBron James, or the site of Sojourner Truth's "Ain't I a Woman" speech in 1851. But not until Zaila Avant-garde, a black girl from Harvey, Louisiana, won the Scripps National Spelling Bee in 2021 did I hear of another of my hometown's claims to fame: Akronite MacNolia Cox was the first black student to make it to the final round of the National Spelling Bee—in 1936.

Today the Scripps National Spelling Bee is among the most

diverse academic competitions around, but in Cox's day, vicious segregation marred her ascent to the national stage. Poet A. Van Jordan, another Akron native, excavated Cox's incredible story by obtaining information at the city's Department of Vital Statistics and snippets from Cox's mother's diary, which had been preserved by a family member. Cox had to ride in segregated train cars, take back stairs, enter banquets through the kitchen, and stay at the home of a black surgeon in D.C. because the Willard Hotel, where the other spellers stayed, wouldn't welcome her.

Cox spelled flawlessly in round after round of the national competition. Meanwhile her white competitors misspelled words and were allowed to remain in the competition due to technicalities. When she looked destined to win, spelling bee officials gave her a word that wasn't on the approved list: *Nemesis*, the name of the Greek goddess of divine retribution and revenge, a proper noun and, by the competition's own laws at the time, verboten. She spelled it incorrectly and was knocked out of the competition. She went home to Ohio, where scholarships she'd been promised never materialized, and she died of cancer, a domestic, at age 53.

Jordan's poetic retelling of her story, *M-A-C-N-O-L-I-A*, published in 2006, tells Cox's life story in reverse from her deathbed to the night before the historic spelling bee, the moment of her highest potential. In an article, "The Word Is 'Nemesis': The Fight to Integrate the National Spelling Bee," historian Cynthia Greenlee captures the larger significance of the story. "Historically, African-Americans have understood the spelling bee as a contested racial space, where mastering a word list was a feat of skill, motivation, and racial resistance through direct competition with one's 'social betters,'" she writes. "If black spellers weren't actually sparring with white rivals, each word memorized—the letters, language of origin, possible meanings—was another symbolic brick building a black community hungry for the book-learning denied to them in slavery and segregation."

Much of the media coverage of Avant-garde's victory noted contemporary injustices that result in few black competitive spellers—expensive travel costs and competition fees, lack of sponsorships, and the fact that schools with many black children have fewer resources to support and train students. And it's true that coaches like the fictional English professor Dr. Larabee in the movie *Akeelah and the Bee* are scarce and pricey. Many former Scripps Bee winners and finalists charge more than $100 an hour to groom the next generation of competitors.

But the inequity is deeper and longer-standing than mere access to a spelling bee. And Avant-garde, a homeschooled phenom and three-time Guinness World Record holder for basketball dribbling, is the kind of exception that accentuates the rule. She had to be extraordinary in so many ways to win her national title. The average child in America today—black or white—lacks access to spelling instruction itself, let alone opportunity for in-depth study of letter patterns, language nuances, and word meanings.

Four Things Parents Need to Know About Spelling

As adults, we know that the professional world judges spelling mistakes severely. Errors in job applications and résumés tend to bias recruiters against candidates and harm career advancement, studies show. What we may not fully appreciate is that the consequences of spelling woes emerge in elementary school, long before students enter the workforce.

Here are four things you need to know now about how spelling impacts your child—and how you can impact their spelling:

SPELLING IS INTEGRAL TO DEVELOPING INTO A READER AND WRITER. Spelling is the glue that sticks words in memory, renders them instantly recognizable in print, and makes reading them quicker and more fluent. Research studies suggest that the more accurate and stable your memory of a word's spelling, the faster you'll read the word. Spelling knowledge has been directly linked to reading fluency, and even third-grade reading achievement scores. And evidence suggests that explicit spelling instruction improves students' spelling, as you would expect, while also supporting better phonological awareness and reading skills.

SPELLING ERRORS NEGATIVELY BIAS TEACHER ASSESSMENTS IN SCHOOLS, EVEN WHEN THAT'S NOT THE FOCUS OF THEIR GRADING. Appearances matter so much that it's hard for teachers to separate the content of student writing (the knowledge it displays, the arguments it makes, and the quality of the supporting evidence) from its presentation (handwriting, spelling, and grammar). Teachers have difficulty fairly and validly viewing the substance of work that has spelling issues. Thus, students who struggle with spelling are at risk of receiving lower grades in other subjects and having their competency overlooked.

SPELLING IS GENERALLY NEGLECTED IN SCHOOLS. Researchers have described spelling instruction as "the abandoned stepchild in the family of language arts." Many teachers devote minimal minutes to it per day, even though many students experience substantial spelling difficulty, by teachers' own reports. Others spend considerable time on spelling instruction but rely on practices that they know don't work. Still others outsource instruction to online apps of questionable quality. In numerous surveys, the vast majority of elementary school teachers say spelling is inadequately addressed in the curriculum.

PARENTS CAN MAKE A HUGE DIFFERENCE. As with so many other areas of literacy development, parents are particularly well positioned to spur this high-impact skill. You can facilitate regular exposure to print that helps your child pick up on patterns on their own and you can teach spelling directly. And remember, even if you're not a spelling champ, your skills are surely better than your preschooler's.

Through the years, you'll observe volumes of your child's authentic writing in the lists, letters, and stories they pen at home. These are great fodder to identify the words your child wants to use, those they struggle with, and those you should teach next. (If you're ready to assess their spelling chops and they haven't written anything at home lately, suggest they draw up a birthday or present wish list or write to a relative.)

Free from the confines of rigid school schedules, you have more time than teachers to instruct your child on the spellings of individual words. You're also a ready resource to respond to in-the-moment spelling questions and challenges that pop up. This doesn't mean hours of drills or forgoing more relaxed playtime: a little spelling instruction, offered consistently, goes a long way.

How Parents Can Spur Spelling

Successful storytime means a comfy setting, good books, and page-turning performances. By comparison, spelling with your child feels stripped down, a cappella rather than musical theater. There's no deferring to an author's words, an illustrator's images, or a character's voice to guide the lessons or drive engagement. Still, talking about words and segmenting them into letters can bring a mindfulness, care, and engagement to family life that's just as vital and powerful as a read-aloud.

Parents have ample occasion, through the days and years, to meaningfully explore and cultivate spelling with our children. We've got the time—even if it doesn't always feel that way—and can build the expertise to teach our kids fruitful strategies, encourage their interest in words, and help them become more reflective and analytical about their writing. Here are eight ways to support strong spelling at home:

CONSISTENTLY DRAW ATTENTION TO PRINT. Kids learn a lot about spelling without being explicitly taught, and this learning begins as soon as they pay attention to written words, typically around 3 years old. Their environments—the books, signs, and other text around—provide the raw material for subconscious learning. Whenever kids lock in on the letters in books, on signs, on toys, and elsewhere, they soak up and analyze visual characteristics of written language.

Kids instinctively pick up the relative frequency of different letter combinations from repeated exposure to writing in their environment, and they apply this statistical knowledge to even their earliest spelling attempts. This unconscious awareness of visual patterns in spelling develops long before they learn that letters represent speech sounds or start trying to spell phonetically. For example, preschoolers tend to write common letters (e.g., E, T, and A) more often than infrequent ones (e.g., J, Q, and Z) in those seemingly random strings of letters they produce early on. Letters from their own names, and letter combinations in alphabetic order, are overrepresented in their scribblings. Their writing attempts reflect the print they've noticed most and what the people in their lives have taught them.

Researchers call this process *statistical learning,* because these spelling efforts are informed by how frequently a child has seen letters appear in certain combinations, orders, and positions. Children aren't consciously counting the instances of certain sequences or calculating probabilities, but they've gathered the data and synthesized it to inform their own writing, nonetheless. And the more complex, contextual, or rare the pattern, the harder it is and longer it takes to grasp subconsciously. Patterns that exist in one circumstance but not another are especially tricky. (Think of spelling the short /o/ sound with an A after W or QU—like in *swab, squad,* or *wallet*—but spelling it with O otherwise—like in *odd, body,* or *olive*).

Parents aid statistical learning by facilitating lots of exposure to print. In the beginning, this requires an adult directing the child—for instance, pointing to the text accompanying an illustration in a picture book, or to their name on a piece of paper.

ENCOURAGE WRITING. Although spelling bee contestants spell aloud to demonstrate their mastery, your child's earliest attempts will likely be on paper. Nurture their writing by always having paper and crayons or colored pencils on hand for them to scribble away long before they can write letters we'd recognize. It's a joy to behold the creations that a stack of index cards and a pencil in the back seat of the car can inspire.

Children as young as 2 or 3 years old demonstrate some knowledge of writing, even if they have no idea yet that it connects with spoken language. Pretend-writing grocery lists, restaurant menus, signs, and so on as a part of play at home is a precursor to spelling, too. One day you may notice that those scribbles are running from left to right and top to bottom on the page. Another day some conventional-looking letters may start popping up amid the slashes and squiggles.

You can ask your child what their writing says and even transcribe a traditional version of it below their scribbles. *Way to write! What does this say? I see. I would write that this way: The dog is happy.* (Point to each word as you say it.) Bonus: you get a record of funny stories to revisit and share as they grow.

APPLAUD EARLY SPELLING. The early quality of your child's spelling reflects things we've been talking about throughout this book: their phonemic awareness, their letter knowledge, and the associations they make between the two. With reading, the letters are given to them and they have to sift through their knowledge of a limited set of sounds to approximate a pronunciation. With spelling, they're hearing a word, segmenting the sounds, and settling on one letter sequence from numerous possible combinations.

A child's first attempts at spelling specific words may be wild. They might spell *kit* A-G-H, for example. They understand that writing conveys a message, but they don't yet grasp the details of the connections between letters and sounds. And that's okay. Don't even bother correcting it. Remember that earlier we explored the value of praising the process. Say *I see you are working hard on your letters and writing* and move on. The child in this scenario needs letter-sound work, not spelling lessons.

Once a child understands that letters represent sounds and they have some knowledge of both letters and sounds, their spelling will evolve. They may spell *kit* with a K alone if they've got the initial sound down or K-T if they grasp the starting and ending sounds. You'll know they've progressed, and your approach can evolve, too. Then you can say something like *You listened well to the sounds in* kit. *You've written the letters that say the sounds at the beginning and end of* kit. *Do you hear the middle sound in* kit, *too? I hear an /i/.* Kit *is spelled K-I-T.* (Write each letter as you say it.)

Giving kids the freedom to invent their own spellings doesn't interfere with their ability to learn conventional spellings later. In fact, researchers say the exact opposite is true: "Allowing children to engage in the analytical process of invented spelling, followed by appropriate feedback, has been found to facilitate learning to read and spell, not hamper the process."

LOOK FOR THE KNOWLEDGE THEY DEMONSTRATE. Parents' assessments of kids' spelling usually amount to deeming an attempt right or wrong. But that black-and-white thinking doesn't serve kids. To teach, we have to learn to see shades of gray. In this context, that means looking at misspellings with an eye for what kids know about sounds, letters, and the relationships between them. Get in the habit of asking yourself what's "right" within a misspelling. Does the writing show conventional letters? Is the initial sound of the word represented (e.g., spelling *love* with L-V)? Are all the sounds represented? Are some letters in the proper sequence? This kind of analysis of your child's spelling is your window into their knowledge base.

And while it's convenient to envision learners progressing through set phases—say, from spelling phonetically to applying spelling patterns to taking word meaning and word origin into consideration—they don't. The process is much messier. You'll need to make your assessments word by word because kids show some knowledge of letter sequences before they learn how letters and sounds connect. They spell some words flawlessly from the start because of the experiences they've had and the attention they've paid to them. All kinds of factors play a role in their learning, from the complexity of the word to the exposures they've had to it and the lessons they've received in relevant letter sequences and spelling patterns.

Understand that the journey isn't linear, try to grasp where your child is with the particular words they are trying to spell, and you'll get a better sense of how you can help. Praise and support every step on the path, and the rest will come.

Here's an example to illustrate what different spellings of a word might reveal about a child's knowledge and what a parent might say or do to affirm it. We'll get into more specifics about what kids are expected to know by kindergarten and after toward the end of this chapter.

EXAMPLE OF HOW SPELLING THE WORD *BABIES* MIGHT CHANGE OVER TIME

DESCRIPTION	CHILD SPELLING	PARENT RESPONSE
Scribbles. Writing but without conventional letters. No grasp of the connections between letters and sounds.		*Great job working on your writing.*
Seemingly random letters. Shows some awareness of letters versus numbers and other written symbols, but doesn't yet connect them to sounds. May reflect statistical knowledge about the likelihood of certain letter combinations, but not the sounds in the word.	ARG	*I see the letters A, R, and G. You are working hard on your writing.*
Initial sound represented. Makes a clear connection between the initial sound in the word and the letter that represents it.	B	*Yes, babies starts with the letter B. B says /b/.*
One or more letters in proper sequence. Showing awareness of letter-sound connections beyond the first letter.	BA	*Yes, babies starts with the letters B and A. I see you wrote a B and an A. Way to put the letters in order!*

EXAMPLE OF HOW SPELLING THE WORD *BABIES* **MIGHT CHANGE OVER TIME** *(CONTINUED)*

DESCRIPTION	CHILD SPELLING	PARENT RESPONSE
All phonemes represented, but some vowels or consonants may be off. Demonstrates strong phonemic awareness and uses a letter to indicate each sound within the word.	BABEZ	*You have written all of the sounds in* babies. Babies *does start with B-A-B!*
Conventional representation. Has full command of the alphabetic principle and has strong familiarity with common nonphonetic spelling patterns and conventions.	BABIES	*Great job paying attention to all the letters in the word!*

RESPOND TO THEIR QUESTIONS AND INTERESTS. Answering your child's questions about words and exploring words they want to write should be central to your instruction. Kids learn to spell in part through continuous attention to the print they encounter (and produce) in regular life. As you go about your day, be alert to words that exemplify concepts and patterns that are ripe for review or introduction. These could be in recipes, street signs, reading for pleasure, or eventually in homework.

When my daughter was little, I read the stories, notes, and lists she wrote at school and at home and (subtly) kept a running list on my phone of the words she misspelled. I then made a point to spend some time casually teaching them. Depending on the word, I might tell a story about its origin, relate it to a word she spelled correctly, point to some environmental print with the correct spelling, or give a quick lesson in the patterns it embodied.

For example, if your little one is making a menu for a Father's Day breakfast and spells *eggs* with E-G-S, you could praise how well they heard each sound and add that egg has two Gs. Then you could point to the Gs on the egg carton to reaffirm the point.

Any word your child has used in their writing is a great point of departure for discussion. It's of clear practical importance to them because *they* chose to use it. You can tap into that interest and create a teachable moment.

TALK ABOUT *MEANINGFUL* UNITS WITHIN WORDS. Some spelling programs treat the meaning-carrying units within words like suffixes and prefixes as advanced word content for kids to tackle later in elementary school or even middle school. The truth is, though, that many of these elements are well within the grasp of younger children. You could say to a kindergartner: *When you put* un *in front of some words, it means the opposite of the main word.* Unsafe *means not safe.* Unsure *means not sure.* From there, they can apply the idea in all kinds of ways and tell you about the unhappy kid on the playground or a character who celebrated an "unbirthday" in a story they read.

Similarly, you can share that *less* means without a particular quality. You could say: *When you put* less *at the end of some words, it means it isn't that way.* Careless *means not with care.* Hopeless *means not with hope.*

The takeaway here is that even seemingly advanced topics have accessible on-ramps that you can use to ease your child into greater knowledge and skills.

TEACH HELPFUL PATTERNS. The sound awareness and letter knowledge we explored in previous chapters give kids the experience and insights they need to apply the alphabetic principle and spell straightforward words easily. But there are twenty-six letters and forty-four speech sounds in English. There are also 250 or more ways to spell those sounds. Silent letters, single letters representing multiple sounds, and a slew of sounds with the same pronunciation, but different spellings, all make English special.

When there are multiple plausible options, spellers need more than letter-sound knowledge to choose the correct one. Sometimes experience, in the form of that unconscious statistical learning I discussed earlier, comes to the rescue, and kids just pick up the spelling from repeated exposure to it without conscious instruction or analysis. But there are also occasions when a quick lesson from Mom or Dad on spelling patterns can help with questions such as when the /f/ sound is represented by PH or when G goes silent in *sign* and *night*.

Researchers have identified a few helpful categories of patterns to consider. These include letters whose pronunciation may change depending on the surrounding letters or sounds, sequences that are more common in certain positions within words, and cases where meaning factors in. If you know a pattern, teach it. And when you don't, look it up and teach it later. More on that in the next section.

LEARN AS YOU GO. If you're thinking you don't have the knowledge necessary to teach your child spelling patterns, you're not alone. There are lots of ways to gain it, and they don't require reading a textbook from cover to cover or enrolling in grad school. Pick up a copy of an accessible reference book to dip into whenever you want to clarify something—like when C makes a soft sound, as in *cent, cinch,* or *cycle* (when it precedes E, I, and Y) and when it's hard, as in *car, come,* and *curtain* (when it precedes A, O, and U).

You can also take small actions to slowly accumulate language tidbits to draw on when your child asks how something is spelled—or why. For example, you might follow Merriam-Webster Dictionary and Scripps Spelling Bee on Instagram, sign up for a word-origin newsletter, or subscribe to a linguist's podcast. Most parents don't have time to do a deep dive into word histories (nor is it necessary), so it's best to find ways to add a steady trickle of insights into the media diet you already consume. Visit readingforourlives.com/spelling for my latest recommendations of spelling reference books, podcasts, and websites.

Can You Spell C-O-N-V-E-R-S-A-T-I-O-N?

Young kids love a good tale and can appreciate the stories behind how words come into existence. That history brings spelling to life, makes teaching time more fun, and helps answer the perpetual question of why many words aren't spelled the way they sound. Plus, stories make spellings stick in our memories better than just staring at or copying words. Here's a quick list of typical ways words get their spellings. Use it to jump-start your and your child's curiosity and back-and-forth discussion around individual words and their components.

1. **Absorption.** English swallows words from other languages whole, spelling included, especially where food is concerned. *Quiche, pizza, tortilla*, anyone? Over time and with instruction, kids can recognize that words

derived from certain places tend to spell sounds a certain way—such as French-derived words using CH for /sh/, as in *chalet*, *chauffeur*, and *chivalry*.

When dining out or visiting specialty food markets, point out spelling trends you observe. *Look at all the double Ts on this menu:* biscotti, spaghetti, bruschetta, ciabatta*!* (Point to the words.) When playing restaurant at home, order up something tasty and deliver a side of spelling by making a pretend menu and sharing how the items are spelled and why.

2. **Compounding.** Putting two independent words together to form a new one is a nearly universal method of creating more complex words, across languages. But the meanings of some pairings are more transparent than others. Think *doorbell* versus *hogwash*. When kids recognize that a rattlesnake is a snake that rattles, they have a better shot at spelling it right than if they approached it letter by letter.

These examples are easy to point out to kids during routine activities. Parents might say: *Sometimes we put two words together to make a new word. For example,* after *and* noon *make* afternoon. Bed *and* room *make* bedroom. Birth *and* day *make* birthday. *When you're spelling words like these, think of the smaller words inside and spell those.*

3. **Imitation.** The spellings of some words, *onomatopoeias,* are influenced by the sound of the item or action they refer to. Think of comic book favorites like *boom*, *pow*,

and *splat* or *hiss*, *ping*, and *whack*. Some, like *cuckoo*, have been present with various spellings since Middle English.

This is a playful type of word to introduce to young children. Tell them, for example: Onomatopoeia *is such a fun word. This kind of word gets its name by imitating a natural sound. For example, the word* buzz *sounds like a bee's buzz and the word* hiss *sounds like a snake's hiss. When we sing "Old McDonald Had a Farm," all those sounds—the cow's moo, the chick's cluck, and the pig's oink—are onomatopoeias!*

Picture books often mirror the dynamism of onomatopoeias by using bright, bold, exaggerated fonts to accent the key words. Use the vividness of the special fonts to capture your little one's attention and bring focus to letter sequences.

4. Naming. English takes names and turns them into words, too. Called *eponyms*, these name-inspired words include *leotard*, *hypnosis*, and *Mary Janes*. *Proprietary eponyms* include words like *Kleenex*, *Post-it*, *Crock-Pot*, and *Breathalyzer*. They were born of brands that got so popular that their names came to stand in for the whole product class.

Creating words from names is particularly prevalent in medicine, where diseases, symptoms, and tests are often christened after their supposed discoverers, such as Alzheimer's disease, Hodgkin's lymphoma, and Crohn's disease. (Fun fact: Some physicians think it's time to abandon eponyms because they don't describe conditions as well as more scientific names and they don't reflect the group effort involved in medical discovery.)

When you come across these special words, point them out to your child: *The dress code says that you have to wear Mary Janes with your uniform. Mary Janes are dress shoes with a strap across the top. They got their name from a girl named Mary Jane in a popular comic strip.*

Telling the origin stories of words doesn't always directly teach much about the spelling, but it does create a fresh opportunity for your child to look at and ponder the word in question. And time and attention paid to words aids learning for sure.

5. Abbreviation. Collections of initials, or *acronyms*, can be pronounced either letter by letter, like *CNN* (Cable News Network), or as single words, like *NASA* (National Aeronautics and Space Administration) or *GOAT* (greatest of all time). Words can also be shortened by dropping off the end, such as *adorbs* for *adorable* and *rando* for *random*.

Again, these are types of words and terms you'll come across often with your kids. Don't assume they know what they mean. Instead, explain, for example, *The* USA *in* Team USA *stands for United States of America. You spell* USA *just like it sounds—U-S-A. Just be sure to capitalize each letter.*

6. Blending. Combining parts of two words to create a new one has given us *frenemy* (friend + enemy), *glamping* (glamour + camping), and *cosplay* (costume + play). In

Through the Looking-Glass, author Lewis Carroll named the blends that he created—like *mimsy* (miserable + flimsy) and *slithy* (lithe + slimy)—*portmanteaus*, after stiff leather suitcases that opened into two compartments.

Blends show up regularly when *Merriam-Webster* releases lists of new words and definitions it's adding to its dictionary. You could tell your child: Fauxhawk *was just added to the dictionary. It's a combination of* faux, *which means false, and* Mohawk, *which is a haircut where the sides are shaved and the remaining hair is upright down the middle of the scalp. With a fauxhawk, the hair could be gathered or slicked up to the middle instead of being completely shaved off.* Faux *is spelled F-A-U-X.*

7. **Repurposing.** Taking an existing word and giving it a new meaning is yet another way to make a new word. Technologies are frequent culprits. *Tablet, catfish, block,* even *copy* and *paste* all have taken on fresh meanings in the internet era while maintaining the familiar spellings.

You can tell your child, *The word* cloud *is spelled C-L-O-U-D whether you're talking about the water vapor floating high in the sky or the place where your online photos, videos, and music are stored. When people created software that could be delivered through the internet, they used the image of a cloud to represent the big network they hoped to create. The name stuck.*

Use backstories and explanations like these to keep conversations about words and language going in your home. The attention you call to individual words and the letters within them will create fodder for your child's statistical learning and benefit their direct instruction, too.

Pace Yourself

Unlike many subject areas we've covered, there's no consensus as yet on the best order of spelling instruction. While working one-on-one with your child, look to state standards and early-learning guides for what to teach when, but *not* for how fast to move along. With a typically developing child, unhindered by the time and attention constraints of a classroom setting, you'll likely be able to move at a faster clip than a teacher can in an academic year. Additionally, you'll be able to introduce layers of word origin, history, meaning, and structure from the start.

Here's a partial list of the spelling knowledge and skills kids should attain grade by grade, culled from state standards and expert recommendations. Again, keep in mind that the following grade-level designations should be thought of as minimum criteria. Go as fast as your child's interest and knowledge retention allow.

PRESCHOOL
- Makes scribbles and writing with the intent to communicate meaning
- Incorporates letters and familiar words into drawings and artwork
- Forms some letters correctly, although some may be upside down or reversed

- Shows awareness that a letter or cluster of letters represents a word
- Writes using invented spelling—e.g., K-L-K for *clock*

KINDERGARTEN
- Spots, names, and forms letters
- Understands that letters can represent speech sounds in writing
- Writes a letter or letters for most consonant and short-vowel sounds
- Segments and counts the speech sounds within words
- Spells words with regular consonant and vowel sounds, including these common patterns: vowel-consonant or VC (*at*), consonant-vowel-consonant or CVC (*sit*), and consonant-consonant-vowel-consonant or CCVC (*flag*)
- Is able to write some high-frequency phonetically irregular words, such as *of, the, have*

FIRST GRADE
- Distinguishes and spells words with closed syllables (*mat*) and open syllables (*me*)
- Recognizes and uses common long-vowel patterns, such as vowel-consonant-e or VCe (*name, hope, kite*) and combinations of vowels, aka "vowel teams" (*read, seed*)
- Recognizes and uses vowel-r syllable patterns (*burn, car, shirt*)
- Grasps the "floss rule"—that the letters F, L, S, and Z are often doubled after a short vowel at the end of a

word (e.g., *glass, kiss, staff, call, buzz*; exceptions: *bus, yes, this, us*)

- Spells high-frequency irregular words, such as *are, have, what*
- Uses suffixes that mark tense, plurals, and the third person (e.g., *-s, -es, -ed, -ing, -er,* and *-est*)
- Uses prefixes and suffixes that don't change base-word pronunciation or spelling (e.g., *un-, re-, dis-, -ful*)
- Spells compound words with common base words and consistent pronunciation (e.g., *football, Sunday*)
- Spells untaught words phonetically

Check out your own state's standards for reference. Then look for opportunities to spend a few minutes now and then nurturing the skills most relevant to your child. For example, with a beginner, you can snag a piece of paper and write a VC, CVC, or CCVC word (e.g., *at, bat,* or *chat*) on it, then tell your child what you know about it. You might say: *When C and H are together, they can say /ch/, like in* cheese *and* chair. *Can you say /ch/? What happens when you put /ch/ and /at/ together? Yes,* chat. *How would you spell* chat? *Yes, C-H-A-T.*

A Few Lessons from Bee Parents

Beyond the importance of spelling for reading, I love it as a subject for parents to teach because there's great documentation of parents taking young children from spelling novices to masters. The work of parents of kids like 2021 Scripps national champion Zaila Avant-garde offers an interesting (if extreme) case study in literacy-focused parenting. The so-called bee parents that anthropologist and author Shalini Shankar documented in *Beeline: What Spelling Bees Reveal About Generation Z's New Path to Success* place enormous value on education and devote considerable time to supporting their children's learning. So even if our aim isn't to pit our kids against the 476,000 words in *Webster's Third New International Dictionary Unabridged*, there are a few essential lessons we can draw from their approach.

ACT ON YOUR PRIORITIES. Many parents say they value academics, but an honest look at how they spend their time and money may reveal otherwise. Bee parents invest consistently and wholeheartedly in their children's spelling pursuits over many years. Edith Fuller was just 5 years old when she earned a spot in the Scripps National Spelling Bee, helped by her mom quizzing her on words in 20-minute-long sessions throughout the day.

Parents featured in *Beeline* spent hours preparing study materials for their kids. They spent money on dictionaries, word lists, coaching, and travel. Their schedules and budgets demonstrate their commitment.

Again, my point is not that all parents need to go to the lengths that bee parents do, but rather that we can often do more to invest our resources in greater alignment with our intentions for our children.

LEARN ALONGSIDE YOUR CHILD. *Beeline* depicts kids' development from beginner to expert spellers. But parents' growth is on display, too. The book shows parents building the research, teaching, and coaching skills they need to support their children's development. Bee parents are willing to learn, make mistakes, and grow with their kids. They model focus, dedication, and consistency over long periods.

For example, pronunciation is a perennial challenge among bee parents, whether because English is not their first language or the words are rare and seldom spoken. Numerous elite spellers that Shankar interviewed described misspelling words that they knew because they didn't recognize the official pronunciation when it was read aloud at the competition. Their parents had pronounced the words differently during practice (e.g., pronouncing *righteous* as "ri-tee-us"). The kids didn't blame their parents for their errors, but together devised strategies to get better. Parents put in time to learn how to read pronunciation marks and produce the right accents, tones, and stresses.

GET OUT OF THE WAY. Bee parents can't learn the words for their kids. The spellers have to own the work, too, putting in hours and hours of independent study. Elite spellers routinely put in two to four hours of spelling study a day during the week and up to eight hours on holidays and weekends. Avant-garde says she studied seven hours a day to prep for her championship run. As they age from elementary to middle schoolers, they take increasing ownership of the process, devising their own study methods, practice routines, and even software to meet their needs. Ideally, bee parents support without coddling, and their kids learn to persevere with poise and positivity.

Indeed, Shankar, *Beeline*'s author, witnessed Zaila Avant-garde's third-round elimination in the 2019 National Spelling Bee on the word *vagaries*. Two years later, Avant-garde won the cup by correctly spelling *murraya,* a genus of tropical Asiatic and Australian trees. Shankar attributes the elite speller's "astounding progress" to "tremendous work ethic, extraordinary aptitude, and a whole lot of parental investment and support."

Avant-garde credits her dad with noticing and nurturing her spelling gifts. She invested in herself, too, reportedly spending her $10,000 prize winnings from a 2020 online spelling bee to pay for study materials and private tutoring from a past Scripps Bee runner-up. It just goes to show that when we support kids' academic interests, they learn how to get themselves to their own next level.

--- JOURNAL PROMPTS ---

- How would you describe your child's spelling now (e.g., scribbles, random letters, partially phonetic, conventional)?

- What strategies will you use to encourage your child to write every day, from lists and letters to stories and poems?

- Where will you make a note of words that your child is interested in or struggling to spell?

- What are some everyday opportunities you have to point out words and talk about how they are spelled?

10

Pathfinding: How Savvy Parents Keep Learning and Leading

Knowledge is of two kinds. We know a subject ourselves, or we know where we can find information upon it.

—Samuel Johnson

My goal with this book was to write the definitive guide on how to raise a reader. And just by virtue of reading this far, you've gotten up to speed on the scientific consensus that's emerged from high-quality peer-reviewed research. Together, we've built a foundation of facts-based knowledge about how children learn to read. We've separated evidence from anecdote in pursuit of more effective parenting and added a host of powerful tools, exercises, and activities to your literacy-building repertoire.

But truth be told, you're not raising *a* reader in general, you're raising *your* reader. So in addition to core knowledge and universally helpful practices, you need some specific support to help you navigate the next leg of your family's reading journey.

In the throes of daily life, beyond the pages of this book, it's not always perfectly clear where your child is along that journey or what you need to do next to support them. There are times when you're cruising along, having dynamic conversations, sharing engaging books, and teaching key skills in everyday moments. You're not worried about a thing. There are also times when you witness something in your child's speech or reading that doesn't sit well with you and you feel moved to address it. In both cases, some big-picture perspective goes a long way to boosting your peace of mind and enjoyment.

This is where my GPS Framework comes in. It's designed to help you pinpoint your child's precise location on the road to reading and use research, reflection, and expertise to chart your best next moves. It's like a three-point navigation system that relies on **g**uidelines, **p**ersonal observations, and **s**pecialists to help you glean the info and insights you need to know where your child is and how to forge ahead.

GPS: Get Grounded in Guidelines

Well-researched lists of developmental milestones (like those earlier in the book), school readiness checklists, and grade-level learning standards succinctly distill important thinking on what to expect of kids when. They're all invaluable resources for initial monitoring of your child's development. Review them even when you think everything's going fine, to ensure your child is on track. And definitely consult them when you have doubts or concerns—you'll gain the insights needed either to nip issues in the bud or to relieve unfounded worries you have.

This research-bolstered knowledge of what kids typically know or do (or *should* know or do) at particular ages can break you out of the trap of comparing your kids with the limited sample of children in your immediate proximity. Because, let's face it, your little one's siblings, neighbors, and friends make for a pretty small sample size. Plus, knowing about typical development can also lower your stress and anxiety by highlighting your child's strengths and putting their challenges into context.

When you are on top of milestones and expectations, you can detect any issues and reach out for help sooner, which leads to faster diagnoses and earlier access to vital support services. You're also better equipped to have effective conversations with your child's pediatrician, teachers, and any specialists, because you're already familiar with typical development and have better vocabulary to describe what's going on.

Even when your child isn't experiencing any developmental delays or learning issues, knowledge of milestones helps you make better decisions around their education and activities. You'll know what they need to work on or practice most. I also find that this child development insight encourages us to be more attentive, responsive, and (dare I say) patient with our kids, because it tempers our expectations around their attention span and behavior for their age. In other words, it will help ensure that you don't see issues where there are none.

To jump-start monitoring your child's development, I recommend six free resources. But first, a caveat. These guidelines are just a first step in the process of alerting you to potential risks, delays, or concerns. Think of them as reflection prompts for you and conversation starters for checkups with your child's doctor or meetings with their teachers—not the be-all and end-all measure of your journey (more on that below).

1. CDC Guidelines

The Centers for Disease Control and Prevention publishes a list of developmental milestones that is based on evidence and features easily observable skills and behaviors. This makes it a wonderful resource for parents. It covers milestones for kids from 2 months through 5 years old. And it addresses milestones in many areas, including social/emotional development, cognitive development, language/communication development, and physical development. This is an excellent resource to consult for updates and further context to the milestones listed previously in this book.

2. ASHA Guidelines

The American Speech-Language-Hearing Association publishes developmental guidelines that focus on communication, feeding, and swallowing. The communication milestones show the ages by which at least 75 percent of American English–speaking kids have attained a skill. The feeding and swallowing milestones are based on international data and are consistent across languages and countries. ASHA updates its guidelines every five years, so you can be sure the information is relatively current.

3. Reach Out and Read Milestones

Reach Out and Read is a national nonprofit that promotes daily reading with children. They put out a guide on Milestones of Early Literacy Development. It clarifies typical development in motor skills, communication, and cognition for newborns through 5-year-olds. It also gives tips for parents on what to read with kids—and how.

4. State Early Intervention Information

Each state has publicly funded programs that provide free or reduced-cost speech therapy, physical therapy, and other services for children who're at risk for developmental delays and disabilities. They also publish brochures and checklists to help families recognize when their kids need screenings or diagnostic evaluations. These helpful resources tend to be less detailed than the CDC or ASHA guidelines, but they contain more specific contact info to help you access screenings and specialists for your child in your state, if needed.

5. State Early-Learning Guidelines

If you really want to go the extra mile, state governments publish guidelines about early learning, standards for early-childhood education programs, and guidance for families. These documents tend to be long and dense, but they are worth a look for insights into the expectations for infants, toddlers, and preschoolers in your area. For example, my state's early-learning standards are 142 pages long and have sections devoted to early literacy, listening and understanding, speaking and communicating, mathematical thinking, scientific thinking, and much more. You may want to find this resource for your state and save it, rather than trying to dig too far into it right now, especially if your child is on the younger side. And be sure to remember, these kinds of learning standards don't show where kids typically are, but rather where state authorities think they *should* be.

6. State/Common Core Standards

You can also dive into your state's kindergarten standards for a glimpse of what schools will expect of your child. Most U.S. states and territories use Common Core standards. Virginia, Texas, Alaska, Nebraska, Arizona, Oklahoma, Indiana, and South Carolina, on the other hand, have created standards of their own. Like the early-learning standards, these documents don't show what kids typically know or do at a certain age or grade level. They're more aspirational, and they detail what state authorities want kids to achieve at certain points in time. For example, the Common Core kindergarten standards aim for kids to understand one-to-one letter-sound correspondences and know the most frequent sounds for each consonant by the end of kindergarten. They also say kids should be able to read high-frequency words such as *the, of, to, you, she, my, is, are, do,* and *does* by sight.

Sadly, most kids aren't meeting grade-level expectations around reading. This is another reason your child is so fortunate that you're informing yourself about standards now, plus research-backed ways to meet them.

Monitoring your little one's progress isn't a one-and-done exercise. Once you've looked at the relevant guidelines and saved them for future reference, you've got to remind yourself to refer to them as your child grows older. The simplest way to do this is to make a calendar appointment to review them at certain intervals, such as on the first day of each new quarter. If you use a project management system or to-do list app, you could assign this as a task for a particular date as well. You could also use periodic occurrences like your child's birthday or upcoming doctor's appointments as a trigger to take a look at milestones and gather your thoughts.

GPS: Ponder Personal Experience

You're an expert on your child, and that knowledge is maximized when you consciously observe them and purposefully document what you see, hear, and experience. Don't underestimate the power of your perspective. You are truly your child's first line of defense against reading challenges—and the first line of support for getting them where they need to be. You likely will spend more time with your child than anyone else over the years before they start school. After all, moms on average spend 7.5 waking hours a day with their kids under 6 and dads spend about 5.3 hours per day, according to the U.S. Bureau of Labor Statistics. That leaves lots of moments to witness elements of your child's development—way more than your pediatrician can observe in a visit. And if you're not a primary caretaker for your little one, don't fret. Work with whoever is with your child most to make sure they record thoughtful observations.

What you notice can lead to more quickly identifying issues and so more quickly getting your child support when needed, which will smooth their path *a lot*. And that's sorely needed. One out of every six children is diagnosed with developmental disabilities these days, according to the National Health Interview Survey, and issues in physical development, socioemotional development, and language development all impact literacy outcomes.

Observing and documenting your child's milestones will build habits of care and responsiveness that will deepen your emotional bond and nurture their development. Reflecting on your child's growth boosts positive emotions, and documenting it creates a lasting treasure trove of memories. The monitoring doesn't have to feel clinical. It can celebrate the wonder of childhood in the same spirit as filling a twelve-slot picture frame with photos from each month of a child's first year or tracking their height with marks on a wall in your home.

Pay attention to the gut feelings, recurring worries, or even feelings of calm and positivity that are all part of daily life with kids. Write down your observations, including areas where your child seems to be thriving and struggling. List your questions. You can collect all of these thoughts in a paper journal on your nightstand or in a notes app on your phone. Use whatever method is most convenient for you. Just be sure to always note the date. Journaling, however informal, encourages greater self-awareness and self-knowledge, as well as better attention and attunement to your child's journey—not to mention creating a helpful record of your child's milestones and challenges to share with your village when needed.

There's another benefit in documenting your observations about your child's development. Bringing concrete information to appointments with doctors makes the visits easier and more productive. The same is true with any other professionals or specialists you wind up meeting with, from teachers to development pros. When you can share concrete examples about any concerns, you advance the conversation much farther and faster. You provide vital data that the professionals can put into the context of what they know from years of study and experience with hundreds of children. You accelerate the time to secure help if needed or to alleviate your concerns.

Parents are so critical for catching developmental issues in their children that official guidance for pediatricians emphasizes the need to build better, more trusting relationships with parents and to give them clearer written information about milestones. Experts even advocate focusing checkups on parents' concerns, because doing so makes doctor visits more relevant and collaborative.

GPS: Seek Out Specialists

Now, once you're coming from a place of basic knowledge and awareness, if you sense there's an issue in your child's development or you just want to learn more, tap into other people who can help. Seeking out specialists rescues you from having to hunt and peck all over the internet for guidance and likely come up short. A word with someone who really knows the subject matter can get you to more reliable information, and can also teach you the key vocabulary and insights to make any of your own further searching more specific and effective.

Perhaps more important, conversations with an expert any

time you have doubts about your child's development or about their learning progress will save you time and banish overwhelm by quickly clarifying your next steps. The pro may treat the issue directly or refer you to someone else who can. They can go deep fast because they've already put in years of work and study that an inexpert Google search just can't match.

Action is the name of the game, so reach out to real people with real knowledge to eliminate bottlenecks. Instead of trying to figure out what to do yourself, get focused on finding the people who can help you move forward. They've got a well of knowledge from years of study and practice that will save you tremendous time, frustration, and discouragement.

Pediatricians, for example, are an overlooked fount of language and early-literacy knowledge. Most parents simply don't understand the purpose and power of pediatrician visits, so they don't fully leverage that golden face time. The American Academy of Pediatrics recommends thirteen well-child visits before 6 years old, but research suggests that kids miss a third to half of those visits. Parents cite transportation challenges, work schedules, and financial issues as barriers, and clinicians say they see a drop-off when there are no scheduled vaccinations. One doctor observed, "I think there is a sense with some of our patients that if we're not giving a prescription or not giving a vaccine, and we're just talking and weighing and measuring them, that we're not doing anything."

Think of the visits when your child is well and no vaccines are due as your special time to talk about the bigger picture of your child's growth. Sure, the visits are brief (usually less than ten minutes) and you may be sensitive about monopolizing the doctor's time, especially if you've spent a long time in the waiting room yourself. But take the time. Seize the opportunity.

Even if your child seems right on track and you have no developmental concerns, I still recommend taking the time to ask questions about development, screenings, and local resources. You're then better prepared to assess your child both at that time and down the line, and you're also in a great position to help other parents you know who are struggling—and the research indicates there will be some in your circle.

The conventional approach to parent education (winging it with a splash of cursory research) also leaves us woefully underinformed about the access every family has to early intervention services.

Every single state has a federally funded program that offers free and reduced cost services for kids in need. And perhaps unsurprisingly, every state calls it something different. It's Infant & Toddler Connection in Virginia, Early Childhood Intervention in Texas, Birth to 3 in Wisconsin, and so on. Children transitioning out of early intervention programs will get a new assessment by local school districts after turning 3 to see if they qualify for further services. Early intervention program staff start transition plans around age 2.5 to prep families for what's ahead. Children not already receiving early intervention services can be screened and access services, if needed, by contacting the district's special education department once they are 3 or older. Sadly, the vast majority of parents aren't aware of the services or think that they can't afford them.

In addition to local specialists, you can also seek out expert advice and information online. Look up and read about the latest cutting-edge research in terms of what works best to address your particular goals and concerns for your child. Follow education news and child development sites. There is a lot of important and valuable research going on, but you may need to dig a bit to find it—and it's important to understand that it's not all immediately applicable to parenting.

Researchers (who are often parents as well) do make an effort to get their best advice to the people who need it most, but they may take it slow in order to be confident in their results before taking them to the streets. Lisa Scott, a psychology professor and the director of the Brain, Cognition & Development Lab at the University of Florida, says it's important for parents to realize that study results must be replicated before researchers can be sure they're valid, not a fluke or the product of some unknown factor or mistake. For example, she and her team recommended that parents make sure to read books with named characters to infants—but first they conducted no less than *four* studies with different methods to confirm the value of the recommendation. The tweaking and critiquing of methods and analysis in community with other researchers is the point. That's how science and knowledge advance.

"It took me a long time to really be comfortable with being able to give that advice to parents," she told me. Once Scott was ready, though, she hustled to get the word out to parents. She published a piece in The Conversation, a nonprofit independent news outlet devoted to sharing expert views for the public good. She even worked with a filmmaker to put together a mini-sitcom public service announcement about reading books to babies. Her comments have been picked up in media as far-flung as *The Washington Post* and the *New Zealand Herald*. Heck, she's even tweeted about the importance of reading the right books at the right time to benefit babies' brains.

There are a few lessons for parents in this example of bridging from research to practice.

IT'S WORTH YOUR WHILE TO FOLLOW NEW DEVELOPMENTS. Fresh findings with practical implications for raising strong, thriving readers, writers, thinkers, and communicators will continue to emerge as research and technology advance. No single study is gospel, so the way forward is to see new findings not as providing "the answer" but as an opportunity to refine our understanding—and prompt new questions. As health writer Kim Tingley advises, think of a study's value as a slight adjustment of an eyeglass-lens prescription. "Each one answers the question 'Is it clearer like this, or like this?'" she writes, "and in doing so, brings our view of reality—our understanding of ourselves and the world around us—into sharper focus."

RESEARCH JOURNALS LIKELY AREN'T YOUR BEST FIRST STOP. Parents don't have to dive headlong into *Reading Research Quarterly, Review of Educational Research,* or *Scientific Studies of Reading.* Ninety-nine percent of what's found there is not for us. That is, it's the work of researchers writing for researchers, not the public.

Peer-reviewed articles tend to be thick with jargon, statistical analysis, and theoretical concerns that are tough for a layperson to digest. More than that, much of it is preliminary, inconclusive, and not helpful to your immediate project of raising a strong reader and writer. The scholars are publishing their findings not because they are definitive, but because they add to the body of knowledge on a topic by affirming or discrediting other theories or raising areas ripe for further research. Once they are published, more scholars can then weigh in on the rigor of their methods, the persuasiveness of their findings, and their relationship to other relevant studies.

EXPERTS DO DISSEMINATE INFORMATION DIRECTLY TO THE PUBLIC. Scott published in The Conversation, a news outlet that I first learned of when I took part in the OpEd Project's Public Voices program at the University of Texas, which trains underrepresented expert voices to enter public dialogue on critical subjects. During that program, I witnessed professors take great pains to break out of the jargon and conventions of their disciplines to deliver powerful, practical insights to a broad audience.

Some researchers also publish blogs and newsletters in which they share tips and tools for teachers and parents. Other ways to hear directly from experts include watching online recordings of their speeches and presentations, viewing documentaries that feature their work, and reading the guides and books they've published for parents, often in conjunction with research centers at their universities or national early-literacy nonprofits. Visit readingforourlives.com/experts for a roundup of resources featuring my favorite thinkers on early language and literacy.

And that's my GPS framework. It codifies three steps that many savvy parents already think to do *sometimes*—so that you're more likely to repeat them again and again through your parenting years, as you face all manner of challenges, decisions, and issues. You can still consult family and friends, your media of choice, or Google. You'll just also have a handy prompt to ground your thinking in generally accepted milestones and standards; in deep reflection on your child, your family, and your aims; and in the specific expertise of people working in the space.

One mom I spoke to noticed that her son was below age expectations in speech starting at his 9-month doctor's visit. She began monitoring his language development closely. She brought up the issue with his pediatrician and, when he was still behind at 12 months, got a referral to free speech therapy through their county in Colorado.

"For me, taking my own concerns seriously and bringing them up with the pediatrician was key. Then the paperwork to get the evaluation took a while, but I tried to stay on top of that," she explained. "I also think looping in experts does help in this case. We heard a lot of well-meaning family and friends say, 'So-and-so's kid didn't talk at all until she was three, and now she never stops talking' or 'All second children talk late.' Those can be true, but it was also true in our case that our son had a developmental delay that is about more than just words, but about how he communicates with us."

And as you know, from reading this book, it's also about his long-term literacy prospects, because oral-language development is so intimately tied to vocabulary, comprehension, and the language of reading instruction. So take a page from her book, and keep an eye on your child and their road ahead. You'll be glad you did.

JOURNAL PROMPTS

- What will be your go-to sources for information on raising a reader? Do some research and then list the specific websites, newsletters, or publications you intend to follow, including any from this chapter that resonated with you.

- How can you find early-childhood and -literacy organizations in your state or local community? What are the key criteria you will use to assess the quality of news and information about reading that you find in your chosen sources?

- How will you keep all the resources and organizations you discover top of mind? List specific actions like bookmarking their websites, subscribing to their newsletters, following their social media feeds, and so on.

Raising All Readers

Human rights are not things that are put on the table for people to enjoy. These are things you fight for and then you protect.
—Wangari Maathai

It's easy to lose sight of the big picture of your child's journey to reading, writing, and spelling because there's so much learning happening linguistically, cognitively, physically, and socioemotionally along the way. There are babbles and first words, scribbles and writing, letter-sound matches made, and words and sentences read—and understood.

You now have a number of ideas for educating yourself so that you can positively influence your child's literacy trajectory from day one. I've emphasized that there are critical milestones on the road to reading success and mapped the early-literacy terrain to help you gain a deeper, more nuanced understanding of what kids need and how you can provide or facilitate it.

Chapter 1 introduced you to your greatest raise-a-reader superpowers. Chapter 2 showed you what reading development from infancy to early elementary school looks like from the child's perspective. Chapters 3 and 4 outlined six essential reading lessons that parents are uniquely equipped to give, plus some enduring teaching principles to help you stay the course. Chapters 5 through 9 showed you how to spur key reading leaps, including boosting oral vocabulary, discerning sounds in words, grasping the form and function of print, mastering letters, mapping speech to print, and making meaning of it all. And Chapter 10 offered tips for learning as you go. I dug into each topic one by one to help you identify what to do, when, and (most important) how in everyday life with young children.

My hope is that together these chapters illustrate how prioritizing raising a reader gives you something meaningful around which to build your family life. That focus alone will alleviate a host of issues plaguing parents today—struggles to prioritize time and spending, lack of the knowledge and networks to make sound decisions, and failure to get the results you want despite lots of activity. That clarity of purpose also helps you attract the information, people, resources, and experiences you need.

It's impossible to teach your child everything they need to know to thrive in an unpredictable world. But when you focus on reading, you can rest assured that you're building the skill that supports all others. It truly facilitates learning in every other area of life—academically and personally, as workers and as citizens—and is the undisputed best tool to help kids meet the demands of adulthood. It's also a powerful bridge to the best of public life: libraries, schools, and community.

So much of the boredom and monotony that parents complain of in the first years of caregiving comes from our lack of knowledge about all the glorious development that's unfolding for our children. We can sometimes be inattentive and insensitive to the miracle in front of us. But when we know what we're observing, imagine what the child is experiencing, and aim to be responsive, our curiosity, attunement, and enjoyment of parenting grows.

I've endeavored to show you the breadth of your role in your child's life, the depth of their literacy needs, and the insufficiency of school alone to meet them. I hope that you will take what you've learned here and be a voice for good sense, good reason, and good instruction in your local community.

You can become an early-literacy expert in the time it takes to learn and grow in supporting your child's reading journey. You can become the smart voice for change in childcare settings and in schools. You can be the hands and heart that organizes the neighborhood book swap, hosts a toddler talk play group in your backyard, or advocates for everyday literacy wherever you go. You can be the public servant arguing for equity in the PTA, school board, or state legislature.

This isn't everyone's path, as Casey Stockstill, a mom of two and an assistant professor of sociology at Dartmouth College who studies preschool segregation, reminded me. "A lot of parents are having a mental health crisis right now, can't keep food on the table, or are just stressed to the max," she explains. "I think if you're in that spot, trying to parent your own kid with dignity is an activist move. That is amazing and that's the best thing to do."

But if you've found the time to read this book, you are likely a parent with the knowledge and ability to make your mission bigger than a sole focus on your own child. "Parents and non-parents should think of the children in your community as everyone's children to some extent," Stockstill says. "We should care about how they're doing, because they're young and they don't have a lot of power yet. They need us to care about them."

I will never meet the person who inspired me to make advocating for children and families my life's work. She died in 1900 but left a legacy of conviction and quiet service that spoke to me powerfully, mother to mother, across centuries, in the months right after my child was born.

Her name was Lucy Goode Brooks. I walked into Friends Association for Children, the latest iteration of the institution she built, 140 years after she established it. Enslaved in Virginia, Brooks gave birth to nine children and endured the aching tragedy of losing her eldest daughter twice: first to a harrowing sale to a distant plantation and then to death in 1862.

When Emancipation dawned, it brought new sorrows and dislocations for Brooks, who watched the streets of Richmond, Virginia, fill with wandering, homeless children. The orphans were "free" but severed from their families by the chaos and cruelty of slavery and war. They reminded her of the child she'd lost, and she set about making a home for them, establishing Friends' Asylum for Colored Orphans in 1868 with the help of her Ladies' Sewing Circle and a Quaker benefactor.

In the years after Brooks's death, the orphanage morphed into a foster-home placement center for abused and neglected children, then into the early-childhood development center that I visited. Nearly a century and a half after she founded it, I toured the center on a site visit for a women's philanthropic group, in a world that would be in some ways unrecognizable to Brooks and in other ways all too familiar.

Walking its halls as a new mom, I felt at a gut level the unfairness of the world. My daughter had been born into a wealthy, educated household where no time, attention, or resources would be spared to give her every opportunity to live her best life, while across town other children just as worthy of living theirs faced much longer odds.

So I committed then and there to do my best to spread the word about things that really move the needle for kids and to continually empower myself and others to pursue them. This book is a pivotal part of that mission. May we all move with intention and collective power to raise our readers well—which is to say *all* readers.

How to Assess Childcare Providers and Schools from an Early-Literacy Perspective

While this book focuses on things parents can do to build early literacy, it's also critical to ensure that the other teachers and caregivers in your child's life support your little one's language and literacy development. I've compiled a short bonus chapter to give you pointers on what to look for (and ask for) from those who help you care for your child.

Download this chapter at readingforourlives.com/caregivers.

Multimedia Resources

Thank you so much for reading this book. It was a great challenge and honor to assemble helpful resources for caregivers in the thick of raising readers. In addition, I've created some online tutorials and bonus materials to help illustrate points made within these pages. For example, audio provides the best example of how to pronounce English's forty-four phonemes, and video demonstrates conversational turns more vividly than text on a page. To access the book's multimedia and the printable worksheets referenced within chapters, visit www.readingforour lives.com.

Acknowledgments

Much love, gratitude, and a dash of awe to my family for inspiring this early-literacy manual and manifesto. Endless thanks to my daughter, Zora, who ignited my curiosity about raising readers (and has a knack for highlighting the gaps between research "best practices" and real-life parenting); my husband, Shaka, who fully supports the countless hours I spend holed up writing or with my nose in a book; and my parents, who named me after a writer and made me feel publishing was my birthright.

I'm also incredibly grateful to my publisher, Avery, for giving me the chance to update *Reading for Our Lives* to amplify the urgent need for parents to engage in their kids' language and literacy development from the start. Our nation's reading crisis is real, and we need more voices advocating for timely intervention through better parenting education and support, accessible early-childhood programs, and high-quality reading instruction. Most importantly, we need more people actively nurturing and teaching reading. I hope this new edition of the book inspires thousands more parents to take literacy action for their own children—and all children.

Thanks to my paperback editor, Hannah Steigmeyer, for

your patience and enthusiasm. If not for your deadlines, check-ins, and gentle nudges, I'd still be revising. And a big shout-out to the cover designer Nellys Liang, marketing muscle Katie McLeod-English, and the rest of the Avery team for getting this book out into the world.

I also owe a debt of gratitude to Lisa DiMona, my amazing agent. Your early belief in this project was invaluable, and I'm so thankful for your wisdom, guidance, and business savvy.

Endless appreciation to the MayaSmart.com team—Laila Weir, Fernando Bautista, and Steff Ho. Publishing new family literacy activities and book recommendations each week is no small feat! Your support helps me navigate website analytics, email automations, and social media algorithms to reach parents in need of support. Together, we deliver.

Finally, to my dear readers: your emails, reviews, speaking invitations, and in-person feedback mean the world to me. Knowing you've read the book, taken action, and shared it as your go-to baby shower gift fuels this literacy-for-all mission! Keep spreading the book love. The next generation of readers needs it.

Notes

By necessity, by proclivity, and by delight, we all quote.

—Ralph Waldo Emerson

I interviewed a number of experts and consulted a wide array of documents and reports across disciplines from neuroscience, history, and linguistics to psychology, education, and speech therapy. I've included a detailed list of citations here for those who would like to check my work or expand upon it. Inevitably, there are additions and corrections that don't make it into print. If you discover relevant references or attributions, please email me at hello@mayasmart.com so I can set the record straight. A book like this is only as helpful as the sources it relies on, so suggestions for improvements are always welcome.

You can find an updated list of endnote amendments at read ingforourlives.com/endnotes.

INTRODUCTION: WE SHOULD ALL BE READERS

2 **Basic literacy skills among U.S. adults:** OECD, *Time for the U.S. to Reskill?: What the Survey of Adult Skills Says,* OECD Skills Studies (OECD Publishing, 2013), 3, 11–12, https://doi.org/10.1787/9789264204904-en.

2 **unusually persistent across generations:** OECD, *Time for the U.S. to Reskill?,* 3, 11–12.

2 **One in six U.S. adults has low literacy skills:** OECD, *Time for the U.S. to Reskill?*, 11.

2 **36 million U.S. adults:** OECD, *Time for the U.S. to Reskill?*, 33.

2 **can't compare and contrast:** OECD, *Time for the U.S. to Reskill?*, 61.

2 **more likely to pass on weaker skills:** OECD, *Time for the U.S. to Reskill?*, 32–33.

2 **likelihood of incarceration:** *Highlights from the U.S. PIAAC Survey of Incarcerated Adults: Their Skills, Work Experience, Education, and Training* (2016), 5, https://nces.ed.gov/pubs2016/2016040.pdf.

3 **more than a million new neural connections:** Center on the Developing Child at Harvard University, "Brain Architecture," https://developingchild.harvard .edu/science/key-concepts/brain-architecture/; Pat Levitt and Kathie L. Eagleson, "The Ingredients of Healthy Brain and Child Development," *Washington University Journal of Law & Policy* 57 (2018): 79, https:// openscholarship.wustl.edu/law_journal_law_policy/vol57/iss1/9.

3 **in place by around 2 years old:** John H. Gilmore, Rebecca C. Knickmeyer, and Wei Gao, "Imaging Structural and Functional Brain Development in Early Childhood," *Nature Reviews Neuroscience* 19, no. 3 (2018): 123–37, https://doi .org/10.1038/nrn.2018.1.

3 **stimulates brain function and shapes brain structure:** Rachel R. Romeo et al., "Beyond the 30-Million-Word Gap: Children's Conversational Exposure Is Associated with Language-Related Brain Function," *Psychological Science* 29, no. 5 (2018): 700–710, https://doi.org/10.1177/0956797617742725; Rianne Kok et al., "Normal Variation in Early Parental Sensitivity Predicts Child Structural Brain Development," *Journal of the American Academy of Child and Adolescent Psychiatry* 54, no. 10 (2015): 824–31, https://doi.org/10.1016/j.jaac.2015.07.009; Vaheshta Sethna et al., "Mother–Infant Interactions and Regional Brain Volumes in Infancy: An MRI Study," *Brain Structure and Function* 222 (2017): 2379–88, https://doi.org/10.1007/s00429-016-1347-1; A. Rifkin-Graboi et al., "Maternal Sensitivity, Infant Limbic Structure Volume and Functional Connectivity: A Preliminary Study," *Translational Psychiatry* 5 (2015): e668, https://doi.org/10.1038/tp.2015.133.

4 **"significantly lower" emergent literacy:** OECD, *Early Learning and Child Well-Being: A Study of Five-Year-Olds in England, Estonia, and the United States* (OECD Publishing, 2020), https://doi.org/10.1787/3990407f-en.

4 **one-third of a nationally representative sample:** National Center for Education Statistics, "NAEP Report Card: 2019 NAEP Reading Assessment," https://www.nationsreportcard.gov/highlights/reading/2019/.

5 **9- and 13-year-olds have dropped:** National Center for Education Statistics, "NAEP Report Card: NAEP Long-Term Trend Assessment Results: Reading and Mathematics," https://www.nationsreportcard.gov/ltt/reading/student-experiences/?age=13.

5 **14 percent of U.S. 15-year-olds read well enough:** OECD, *Country Note United States: Programme for International Student Assessment (PISA): Results from PISA 2018*, 3, https://www.oecd.org/pisa/publications/PISA2018_CN_USA.pdf; OECD, *21st-Century Readers: Developing Literacy Skills in a Digital World* (PISA, OECD Publishing, 2021), https://doi.org/10.1787/a83d84cb-en.

5 **"never or hardly ever" read for fun:** National Center for Education Statistics, "NAEP Report Card: NAEP Long-Term Trend Assessment Results: Reading and Mathematics."

5 **30 percent of designated "instructional time":** Soheyla Taie, Rebecca Goldring, and Maura Spiegelman, *Characteristics of Public and Private Elementary and Secondary Schools in the United States: Results from the 2017–18 National Teacher and Principal Survey. First Look*, NCES 2019-140 (National Center for Education Statistics, August 2019), 19, https://nces.ed.gov /pubsearch/pubsinfo.asp?pubid=2019140; Ina V. S. Mullis et al., *ePIRLS 2016: International Results in Reading* (TIMSS & PIRLS International Study Center, Lynch School of Education, Boston College, and International Association for the Evaluation of Educational Achievement, 2017), 256, http://pirls2016.org /wp-content/uploads/structure/CompletePDF/P16-PIRLS-International- Results-in-Reading.pdf; Geoffrey Phelps et al., "How Much English Language Arts and Mathematics Instruction Do Students Receive? Investigating Variation in Instructional Time," *Educational Policy* 26, no. 5 (2012): 647–48, https://doi .org/10.1177/0895904811417580; Tina L. Heafner and Paul G. Fitchett, "Tipping the Scales: National Trends of Declining Social Studies Instructional Time in Elementary Schools," *The Journal of Social Studies Research* 36, no. 2 (2012): 190–215.

9 **"the world and the heavens":** Zora Neale Hurston, *Their Eyes Were Watching God: A Novel* (Perennial Library, 1990), 72.

9 **Jabari Asim's *Girl of Mine*:** Jabari Asim, *Girl of Mine* (LB Kids, 2010).

10 **"We die. That may be the meaning of life":** Toni Morrison, Nobel Lecture, December 7, 1993, https://www.nobelprize.org/prizes/literature/1993/morrison /lecture/.

10 **the brain is at its most flexible:** Center on the Developing Child at Harvard University, "InBrief: The Science of Early Childhood Development," 2007, https://developingchild.harvard.edu/resources/inbrief-science-of-ecd/.

13 **predicted their IQ and language skills *ten years later*:** Jill Gilkerson et al., "Language Experience in the Second Year of Life and Language Outcomes in Late Childhood," *Pediatrics* 142, no. 4 (2018): e20174276, https://doi.org/10 .1542/peds.2017-4276.

13 **growing distractions:** Brooke Auxier et al., *Parenting Children in the Age of Screens* (Pew Research Center, July 2020), 11–12, 47–49, 53–62, https://www .pewresearch.org/internet/wp-content/uploads/sites/9/2020/07/PI_2020.07.28 _kids-and-screens_FINAL.pdf; Laura Bornfreund et al., *Supporting Early Learning in America: Policies for a New Decade* (New America, February 2020), 7–11, https://d1y8sb8igg2f8e.cloudfront.net/documents/Supporting_Early _Learning_in_America_FINAL_JZxpW0v.pdf; Jack Cassidy, Evan Ortlieb, and Stephanie Grote-Garcia, "What's Hot in Literacy: New Topics and New Frontiers Are Abuzz," *Literacy Research and Instruction* 60, no. 1 (2021), 4, https://doi.org/10.1080/19388071.2020.1800202; Common Sense Media, "New Report: Parents Spend More Than Nine Hours a Day with Screen Media," press release, December 6, 2016, https://www.commonsensemedia.org /about-us/news/ press-releases/new-report-parents-spend-more-than-nine-hours

-a-day-with-screen-media; The Genius of Play, "When It Comes to Screen Time, Parents Are Just as Guilty as Their Children," press release, October 21, 2019, https://www.prnewswire.com/news-releases/when-it-comes-to-screen-time -parents-are-just-as-guilty-as-their-children-300941553.html.

14 **single best predictor of school achievement:** Amy Pace et al., "Measuring Success: Within and Cross-Domain Predictors of Academic and Social Trajectories in Elementary School," *Early Childhood Research Quarterly* 46 (January 1, 2019): 112–25, https://doi.org/10.1016/j.ecresq.2018.04.001.

14 **four times as likely to drop out:** Donald J. Hernandez, *Double Jeopardy: How Third Grade Reading Skills and Poverty Influence High School Graduation* (The Annie E. Casey Foundation, January 2012), https://www.aecf.org/resources /double-jeopardy.

14 **usually had no effect on reading achievement:** Beth Boulay et al., *Summary of Research Generated by Striving Readers on the Effectiveness of Interventions for Struggling Adolescent Readers* (National Center for Education Evaluation and Regional Assistance, Institute of Education Sciences, U.S. Department of Education, October 2015), 1–8, https://ies.ed.gov/ncee/pubs/20164001 /pdf/20164001.pdf; Rekha Balu et al., *Evaluation of Response to Intervention Practices for Elementary School Reading* (National Center for Education Evaluation and Regional Assistance, Institute of Education Sciences, U.S. Department of Education, November 2015), 87–94, https://ies.ed.gov/ncee /pubs/20164000/pdf/20164000.pdf; Timothy Shanahan, *Shanahan on Literacy* (blog), "How Much Reading Gain Should Be Expected from Reading Interventions?," February 13, 2017, Reading Rockets, https://www. readingrockets.org/blogs/shanahan-literacy/how-much-reading-gain-should-be -expected-reading-interventions.

14 **levels of reading and writing required:** Donald J. Leu et al., "New Literacies: A Dual-Level Theory of the Changing Nature of Literacy, Instruction, and Assessment," *Journal of Education* 197, no. 2 (2017): 1–18, https://doi.org /10.1177/002205741719700202; Richard Murnane, Isabel Sawhill, and Catherine Snow, "Literacy Challenges for the Twenty-First Century: Introducing the Issue," *Future of Children* 22, no. 2 (2012): 3–15, https://doi.org /10.1353/foc.2012.0013; OECD, *Literacy in the Information Age: Final Report of the International Adult Literacy Survey* (OECD and the Minister of Industry, Canada, 2000), 1–11, https://www.oecd-ilibrary.org/social-issues-migration -health/literacy-in-the-information-age_9789264181762-en.

16 **100,000 studies on how children learn to read:** Eunice Kennedy Shriver National Institute of Child Health and Human Development, NIH, DHHS, Child Development and Behavior Branch, *Report of the National Reading Panel, Teaching Children to Read: An Evidence-Based Assessment of the Scientific Research Literature on Reading and Its Implications for Reading Instruction* (U.S. Government Printing Office, 2000), https://www.nichd.nih.gov/publications /pubs/nrp/intro.

18 **"resist the urge to engage in reading instruction":** Daniel T. Willingham, *Raising Kids Who Read: What Parents and Teachers Can Do* (Jossey-Bass/Wiley, 2015), 93.

1: BEYOND BEDTIME STORIES: THE TRUTH ABOUT GETTING KIDS READY TO READ

22 **"Children who were read five books"**: "Reading to Your Child May Give Them a Million More Words, Study Says," WBZ News, April 4, 2019, https://www.cbsnews.com/boston/news/reading-young-children-million-word-gap-health watch-mallika-marshall/

22 **"the single most significant factor"**: "Read 3 Pledge," H-E-B, https://www.heb.com/static-page/Read-3-Pledge.

22 **"The rewards of early reading"**: Meghan Cox Gurdon, *The Enchanted Hour: The Miraculous Power of Reading Aloud in the Age of Distraction* (HarperCollins, 2019), xiv.

24 **"Without a concerted look"**: Dana Suskind, Beth Suskind, and Leslie Lewinter-Suskind, *Thirty Million Words: Building a Child's Brain* (Dutton, 2015), 225.

24 **cognitive function disparities**: Marianne M. Hillemeier et al., "Disparities in the Prevalence of Cognitive Delay: How Early Do They Appear?," *Paediatric and Perinatal Epidemiology* 23, no. 3 (2009): 186–98, https://doi.org/10.1111/j.1365-3016.2008.01006.x.

24 **language processing gaps**: Anne Fernald, Virginia A. Marchman, and Adriana Weisleder, "SES Differences in Language Processing Skill and Vocabulary Are Evident at 18 Months," *Developmental Science* 16, no. 2 (2013): 234–48, https://doi.org/10.1111/desc.12019; Kimberly G. Noble et al., "Socioeconomic Disparities in Neurocognitive Development in the First Two Years of Life," *Developmental Psychobiology* 57, no. 5 (2015): 535–51, https://doi.org/10.1002/dev.21303.

24 *Early talk is our point of greatest leverage*: LENA, *Inside Early Talk* (LENA Foundation, March 2021), 17, https://info.lena.org/inside-early-talk.

24 **back-and-forth dialogue with adults**: Jill Gilkerson et al., "Language Experience in the Second Year of Life and Language Outcomes in Late Childhood," *Pediatrics* 142, no. 4 (2018): e20174276, https://doi.org/10.1542/peds.2017-4276.

25 **the greater the activity in the brain region**: Rachel R. Romeo et al., "Beyond the 30-Million-Word Gap: Children's Conversational Exposure Is Associated with Language-Related Brain Function," *Psychological Science* 29, no. 5 (2018): 700–710, https://doi.org/10.1177/0956797617742725.

25 **changes the *physical structure* of the brain**: Rachel R. Romeo et al., "Language Exposure Relates to Structural Neural Connectivity in Childhood," *Journal of Neuroscience* 38, no. 36 (2018): 7870–77, https://doi.org/10.1523/JNEUROSCI.0484-18.2018.

25 **drive parents to chronic distraction**: Erika Christakis, "The Dangers of Distracted Parenting," *The Atlantic*, July/August 2018, https://www.theatlantic.com/magazine/archive/2018/07/the-dangers-of-distracted-parenting/561752/.

26 **no health professional**: Dana L. Suskind et al., "Educating Parents About Infant Language Development: A Randomized Controlled Trial," *Clinical Pediatrics* 57, no. 8 (2018): 945–53, https://doi.org/10.1177/0009922817737079.

26 **overall language ability**: Rachel I. Mayberry, Alex A. del Giudice, and Amy M. Lieberman, "Reading Achievement in Relation to Phonological Coding and

Awareness in Deaf Readers: A Meta-Analysis," *Journal of Deaf Studies and Deaf Education* 16, no. 2 (2011): 164–88, https:// academic.oup.com/jdsde/article /16/2/164/364821.

26 **its own syntax and grammar:** "American Sign Language," National Institute on Deafness and Other Communication Disorders, October 29, 2021, https:// www.nidcd.nih.gov/health/american-sign-language.

26 **Skilled deaf signers are often better readers:** Carol Padden and Claire Ramsey, "American Sign Language and Reading Ability in Deaf Children," in *Language Acquisition by Eye*, eds. Charlene Chamberlain, Jill Morford, and Rachel Mayberry (Lawrence Erlbaum Associates, 2000), 221–59.

27 **"the single most important activity":** Julie Dwyer and Susan B. Neuman, "Selecting Books for Children Birth Through Four: A Developmental Approach," *Early Childhood Education Journal* 35, no. 6 (2008): 489–94, https://doi.org/10.1007/s10643-008-0236-5.

28 **more complex and varied words:** Jessica L. Montag, Michael N. Jones, and Linda B. Smith, "The Words Children Hear: Picture Books and the Statistics for Language Learning," *Psychological Science* 26, no. 9 (2015): 1489–96, https:// doi.org/10.1177/0956797615594361.

28 **associated with better literacy, numeracy:** Joanna Sikora, M.D.R. Evans, and Jonathan Kelley, "Scholarly Culture: How Books in Adolescence Enhance Adult Literacy, Numeracy and Technology Skills in 31 Societies," *Social Science Research* 77 (2019): 1–15, https://doi.org/10.1016/j.ssresearch.2018.10.003.

28 **held across pooled data:** Sikora, Evans, and Kelley, "Scholarly Culture."

28 **"the benefits of bookishness":** Sikora, Evans, and Kelley, "Scholarly Culture."

29 **intentional, direct instruction:** Anne Castles, Kathleen Rastle, and Kate Nation, "Ending the Reading Wars: Reading Acquisition from Novice to Expert," *Psychological Science in the Public Interest* 19, no. 1 (2018): 5–51, https://doi.org/10.1177/1529100618772271.

32 **side by side with a mom:** Catherine Compton-Lilly and Anne Delbridge, "What Can Parents Tell Us About Poverty and Literacy Learning? Listening to Parents over Time," *Journal of Adolescent & Adult Literacy* 62, no. 5 (2019): 531–39, https://doi.org/10.1002/jaal.923.

35 **high-interest loan:** Highlite Education Loans, "Tutoring Financing & Education Loans," https://highliteloans.com/.

35 **"explosion in demand" for preschool tutoring:** Douglas Belkin and Globe Staff, "Bringing Up Einstein: Tutor Businesses Tap into a Growing Market: Preschoolers," *Boston Globe*, February 19, 2006; Marek Fuchs, "Education: Tutoring Gives Pupils an Edge . . . for Preschool," *New York Times*, July 31, 2002.

35 **continue to boom:** "Tutoring & Driving Schools in the US," IBISWorld, April 2023.

38 **NAEYC recommends:** "Principles of Effective Family Engagement," NAEYC, https://www.naeyc.org/resources/topics/family-engagement/principles.

39 **teach parents about education issues:** "Family Leadership Institute," City Forward Collective, https://www.cityforwardcollective.org/family-leadership -institute.

2: THE LONG RUN: MILESTONES AND LITERACY TARGETS TO WATCH

45 **millions of years ago:** Rachel Gutman-Wei, "A 'Mic Drop' on a Theory of Language Evolution," *The Atlantic,* December 12, 2019, https://www .theatlantic.com/science/archive/2019/12/when-did-ancient-humans-start -speak/603484/.

45 **most monolingual children:** "Communication Milestones: Age Ranges," American Speech-Language-Hearing Association, https://www.asha.org/public /developmental-milestones/communication-milestones/.

45 **much more recently in human evolution:** Roger D. Woodard, "Writing Systems," in *International Encyclopedia of the Social & Behavioral Sciences,* 2nd ed., ed. James D. Wright (Elsevier, 2015), 773–74, https://doi.org/10.1016 /B978-0-08-097086-8.52027-3.

45 **"recycling" of brain networks:** Stanislas Dehaene, "Evolution of Human Cortical Circuits for Reading and Arithmetic: The 'Neuronal Recycling' Hypothesis," in *From Monkey Brain to Human Brain: A Fyssen Foundation Symposium,* eds. Stanislas Dehaene, Jean-René Duhamel, Marc D. Hauser, and Giacomo Rizzolatti (MIT Press, 2005), 141–151; Stanislas Dehaene and Laurent Cohen, "Cultural Recycling of Cortical Maps," *Neuron* 56, no. 2 (2007): 384–390, https://doi.org/10.1016/j.neuron.2007.10.004.

47 **before birth:** Anthony J. DeCasper and Melanie J. Spence, "Prenatal Maternal Speech Influences Newborns' Perception of Speech Sounds," *Infant Behavior and Development* 9, no. 2 (April–June 1986): 134–148, https://doi .org/10.1016/0163-6383(86)90025-1; P. G. Hepper, D. Scott, and S. Shahidullah, "Newborn and Fetal Response to Maternal Voice," *Journal of Reproductive and Infant Psychology* 11, no. 3 (1993): 148–152, https://doi .org/10.1080/02646839308403210; B. S. Kisilevsky et al., "Fetal Sensitivity to Properties of Maternal Speech and Language," *Infant Behavior and Development* 32, no. 1 (2009): 59–71, https://doi.org/10.1016/j.infbeh.2008.10.002.

47 **By the third trimester of pregnancy:** Carolyn Granier-Deferre et al., "Near-Term Fetuses Process Temporal Features of Speech," *Developmental Science* 14, no. 2 (2011): 340–348, https://doi.org/10.1111/j.1467-7687.2010.00978.x.

47 **contributes to phonetic perception:** Christine Moon, Hugo Lagercrantz, and Patricia K. Kuhl, "Language Experienced in Utero Affects Vowel Perception after Birth: A Two-Country Study," *Acta Paediatrica* 102, no. 2 (2013): 156–60, https://doi.org/10.1111/apa.12098.

47 **"vowels are louder":** Moon, Lagercrantz, and Kuhl, "Language Experienced," 156.

47 **reacted differently to vowel sounds:** Moon, Lagercrantz, and Kuhl, "Language Experienced," 158–59.

48 **"crying is, in fact, nature's way":** Nicola Lathey and Tracey Blake, *Small Talk: How to Develop Your Child's Language Skills from Birth to Age 4* (The Experiment, 2014), 36.

48 **third month of life:** Kathleen Wermke, "Neonatal Crying Behaviors," in *International Encyclopedia of the Social and Behavorial Sciences,* 2nd ed., ed. James D. Wright (Elsevier, 2015), 475, https://doi.org/10.1016/B978-0-08 -097086-8.23106-1.

48 **between 2 and 4 months old:** B. D'Entremont, S. M. J. Hains, and D. W. Muir, "A Demonstration of Gaze Following in 3-to 6-Month-Olds," *Infant Behavior and Development* 20, no. 4 (October–December 1997): 569–571, https://doi.org/10.1016/S0163-6383(97)90048-5; Gustaf Gredebäck, Linn Fikke, and Annika Melinder, "The Development of Joint Visual Attention: A Longitudinal Study of Gaze Following during Interactions with Mothers and Strangers," *Developmental Science* 13, no. 6 (November 2010): 841–847, https://doi.org/10.1111/j.1467-7687.2009.00945.x; Melis Çetinçelik, Caroline F. Rowland, and Tineke M. Snijders, "Do the Eyes Have It? A Systematic Review on the Role of Eye Gaze in Infant Language Development," *Frontiers in Psychology* 11 (2021): 589096, https://doi.org/10.3389/fpsyg.2020.589096.

49 **By 6 months old:** Julie Dwyer and Susan B. Neuman, "Selecting Books for Children Birth Through Four: A Developmental Approach," *Early Childhood Education Journal* 35 (June 2008): 489–94, https://doi.org/10.1007/s10643-008 -0236-5.

49 **right-fit visual and tactile stimulation:** Dwyer and Neuman, "Selecting Books for Children," 490–91.

49 **your baby is driving their own learning:** Jenny R. Saffran, "Statistical Language Learning in Infancy," *Child Development Perspectives* 14, no. 1 (2020): 49–53, https://doi.org/10.1111/cdep.12355.

49 **"Your choice of books":** Caroline J. Blakemore and Barbara Weston Ramirez, *Baby Read-Aloud Basics: Fun and Interactive Ways to Help Your Little One Discover the World of Words* (AMACOM, 2006), 28.

51 **best predictor of expressive vocabulary:** Ed Donnellan et al., "Infants' Intentionally Communicative Vocalizations Elicit Responses from Caregivers and Are the Best Predictors of the Transition to Language: A Longitudinal Investigation of Infants' Vocalizations, Gestures and Word Production," *Developmental Science* 23, no. 1 (2020): e12843, https://doi.org/10.1111/ desc.12843.

51 **better expressive and receptive language skills:** Amber Muhinyi and Meredith L. Rowe, "Shared Reading with Preverbal Infants and Later Language Development," *Journal of Applied Developmental Psychology* 64 (July–September 2019): 101053, https://doi.org/10.1016/j.appdev.2019.101053.

52 **"all the ideas of a toddler":** Susie Allison (@BusyToddler), "Shout out to everyone with a taby this summer," Instagram photo, July 13, 2021, https:// www.instagram.com/p/CRRfy3IrXgL/.

53 **bolster your little one's brain connectivity:** Rachel R. Romeo et al., "Language Exposure Relates to Structural Neural Connectivity in Childhood," *Journal of Neuroscience* 38, no. 36 (2018): 7871–7876, https://doi.org/10.1523 /JNEUROSCI.0484-18.2018; Rachel R. Romeo et al., "Neuroplasticity Associated with Changes in Conversational Turn-Taking Following a Family-Based Intervention," *Developmental Cognitive Neuroscience* 49 (June 2021): 100967, 2–9, https://doi.org/10.1016/j.dcn.2021.100967; Jill Gilkerson et al., "Language Experience in the Second Year of Life and Language Outcomes in Late Childhood," Pediatrics 142, no. 4 (2018): e20174276, 2–9, https://doi .org/10.1542/peds.2017-4276.

55 **may still get clipped:** Linda M. Laila Khan, "A Review of 16 Major
   Phonological Processes," *Language, Speech, and Hearing Services in Schools* 13,
   no. 2 (April 1982): 79–80, https://doi.org/10.1044/0161-1461.1302.77; "Selected
   Phonological Processes (Patterns)*," American Speech-Language-Hearing
   Association, accessed February 3, 2022, https://www.asha.org/practice-portal
   /clinical-topics/articulation-and-phonology/selected-phonological-processes/.

62 **A few quick definitions:** Linnea C. Ehri, "The Science of Learning to Read
   Words: A Case for Systematic Phonics Instruction," *Reading Research Quarterly*
   55, no. S1 (2020): S45–S60, https://doi.org/10.1002/rrq.334.

3: YOU'RE HIRED: ESSENTIAL LESSONS EVERY PARENT CAN—AND SHOULD—GIVE KIDS

67 **since the late fourth millennium BCE:** Roger D. Woodard, "Writing Systems,"
   in *International Encyclopedia of the Social & Behavioral Sciences*, 2nd ed., ed.
   James D. Wright (Elsevier, 2015), 773–74, https://doi.org/10.1016/B978-0-08
   -097086-8.52027-3.

67 **since the sixteenth century:** John Hart, *An Orthographie* (1569; London: Fred
   Pitman, 1850), Google Books.

67 **last several decades:** Keith Rayner et al., "How Psychological Science Informs
   the Teaching of Reading," *Psychological Science in the Public Interest* 2, no. 2
   (2001): 34–74, https://doi.org/10.1111/1529-1006.00004.

68 **critically important for later reading skills:** Christopher J. Lonigan, Stephen
   R. Burgess, and Jason L. Anthony, "Development of Emergent Literacy and
   Early Reading Skills in Preschool Children: Evidence from a Latent-Variable
   Longitudinal Study," *Developmental Psychology* 36, no. 5 (2000): 598–613,
   https://doi.org/10.1037/0012-1649.36.5.596.

68 **preschool and kindergarten screenings:** Marcia Invernizzi et al., "Increased
   Implementation of Emergent Literacy Screening in Pre-Kindergarten," *Early
   Childhood Education Journal* 37 (2010): 437–45, https://doi.org/10.1007
   s10643-009-0371-7; Maura Jones Moyle, John Heilmann, and S. Sue Berman,
   "Assessment of Early Developing Phonological Awareness Skills: A Comparison
   of the Preschool Individual Growth and Development Indicators and the
   Phonological Awareness and Literacy Screening–PreK," *Early Education and
   Development* 24, no. 5 (2013): 668–86, https://doi.org/10.1080/10409289.2012
   .725620; Janelle J. Montroy et al., "The Texas Kindergarten Entry Assessment:
   Development, Psychometrics, and Scale-Up of a Comprehensive Screener," *Early
   Education and Development* 31, no. 5 (2020): 701–38, https://doi.org/10.1080/10
   409289.2020.1726700; Georgenne G. Weisenfeld, Karin Garver, and Katherine
   Hodges, "Federal and State Efforts in the Implementation of Kindergarten
   Entry Assessments (2011–2018)," *Early Education and Development* 31, no. 5
   (2020): 632–52,https://doi.org/10.1080/10409289.2020.1720481.

68 **Mary Walker, born in 1848:** Rita L. Hubbard, *The Oldest Student: How Mary
   Walker Learned to Read* (Schwartz & Wade Books, 2020).

68 **Walker's dream of literacy:** Hubbard, *The Oldest Student.*

68 **"She studied the alphabet":** Hubbard, *The Oldest Student.*

69 **the better their reading comprehension in third grade:** Monique Sénéchal,

Gene Ouellette, and Donna Rodney, "The Misunderstood Giant: On the Predictive Role of Early Vocabulary to Future Reading," in *Handbook of Early Literacy Research*, Vol. 2, eds. David K. Dickinson and Susan B. Neuman (Guilford Press, 2006), 173–82.

69 **the higher their likelihood of graduating from high school:** Donald J. Hernandez, *Double Jeopardy: How Third Grade Reading Skills and Poverty Influence High School Graduation* (The Annie E. Casey Foundation, January 2012), 4–7, https://www.aecf.org/resources/double-jeopardy.

70 **forty "conversational turns" per hour:** LENA Foundation, *Inside Early Talk* (LENA, March 2021), 3–4, https://info.lena.org/inside-early-talk.

70 **"talk pedometer":** LENA Foundation, *Inside Early Talk,* 2.

70 **less than they think they do:** Jeffrey A. Richards et al., "How Much Do Parents Think They Talk to Their Child?," *Journal of Early Intervention* 39, no. 3 (2017): 163–79, https://doi.org/10.1177/1053815117714567.

71 **related to early growth in word-reading skills:** Monica Melby-Lervåg, Solveig-Alma Halaas Lyster, and Charles Hulme, "Phonological Skills and Their Role in Learning to Read: A Meta-Analytic Review," *Psychological Bulletin* 138, no. 2 (2012): 322–52, https://doi.org/10.1037/a0026744.

72 **a causal relationship:** Shayne B. Piasta et al., "Increasing Young Children's Contact with Print During Shared Reading: Longitudinal Effects on Literacy Achievement," *Child Development* 83, no. 3 (2012): 810–20, https://doi.org/10.1111/j.1467-8624.2012.01754.x.

73 **teaching some elements of print in isolation:** Theresa A. Roberts, Patricia F. Vadasy, and Elizabeth A. Sanders, "Preschool Instruction in Letter Names and Sounds: Does Contextualized or Decontextualized Instruction Matter?," *Reading Research Quarterly* 55, no. 4 (2020): 573–600, https://doi.org/10.1002/rrq.284.

73 **distinguish letters from pictures:** Sarah Robins et al., "Parent–Child Conversations About Letters and Pictures," *Reading and Writing* 25 (2012): 2039–59, https://doi.org/10.1007/s11145-011-9344-5.

75 **comprehensive reviews:** National Reading Panel (U.S.), *Teaching Children to Read: An Evidence-Based Assessment of the Scientific Research Literature on Reading and Its Implications for Reading Instruction: Reports of the Subgroups* (National Institute of Child Health and Human Development, 2000), https://www.nichd.nih.gov/sites/default/files/publications/pubs/nrp/Documents/report.pdf; Jim Rose, *Independent Review of the Teaching of Early Reading: Final Report, March 2006* (Nottingham, UK: Department for Education and Skills Publications, 2006), 8, 15–28, https://dera.ioe.ac.uk/5551/2/report.pdf; National Inquiry into the Teaching of Literacy (Australia), Australian Government Department of Education, Science, and Training, *Teaching Reading: Report and Recommendations* (Canberra, Australia: Department of Education, Science, and Training, 2005), 31–38, https://research.acer.edu.au/tll_misc/5/.

77 **a "visible record of language processing":** Reading Rockets, "Louisa Moats: Spelling," YouTube video, April 25, 2014, https://www.youtube.com/watch?v=BjVcR83nAYk.

77 **a view into their understanding:** Gene Ouellette and Monique Sénéchal, "Invented Spelling in Kindergarten as a Predictor of Reading and Spelling in Grade 1: A New Pathway to Literacy, or Just the Same Road, Less Known?," *Developmental Psychology* 53, no. 1 (2017): 77–88, https://doi.org/10.1037/dev0000179.

78 **"Anything that is going to cause trouble":** Reading Rockets, "Louisa Moats: Spelling," YouTube video.

4: YES YOU CAN: FIVE TOUCHSTONES FOR PARENTS WHO DARE TO TEACH

82 **affect kids' language development:** Meredith L. Rowe, "Understanding Socioeconomic Differences in Parents' Speech to Children," *Child Development Perspectives* 12, no. 2 (2018): 122–23, https://doi.org/10.1111/cdep.12271; Zehava Oz Weizman and Catherine E. Snow, "Lexical Output as Related to Children's Vocabulary Acquisition: Effects of Sophisticated Exposure and Support for Meaning," *Developmental Psychology* 37, no. 2 (2001): 265–79, https://doi.org/10.1037/0012-1649.37.2.265; Janellen Huttenlocher et al., "Sources of Variability in Children's Language Growth," *Cognitive Psychology* 61, no. 4 (2010): 343–65, https://doi.org/10.1016/j.cogpsych.2010.08.002.

82 **parent responsiveness:** Catherine S. Tamis-LeMonda, Yana Kuchirko, and Lulu Song, "Why Is Infant Language Learning Facilitated by Parental Responsiveness?," *Current Directions in Psychological Science* 23, no. 2 (2014): 121–26, https://doi.org/10.1177/0963721414522813.

82 **"reciprocal and dynamic interactions":** Jack P. Shonkoff, "Breakthrough Impacts: What Science Tells Us About Supporting Early Childhood Development," *YC Young Children* 72, no. 2 (2017): 8–16, p. 9, http://www.jstor.org/stable/90004117.

83 **conversations about the here and now:** Michael Tomasello and Michael Jeffrey Farrar, "Joint Attention and Early Language," *Child Development* 57, no. 6 (December 1986): 1454–63, https://doi.org/10.2307/1130423; Meredith L. Rowe and Susan Goldin-Meadow, "Differences in Early Gesture Explain SES Disparities in Child Vocabulary Size at School Entry," *Science* 323, no. 5916 (2009): 951–53, https://doi.org/10.1126/science.1167025.

83 **advance infants' language learning:** Erik D. Thiessen, Emily A. Hill, and Jenny R. Saffran, "Infant-Directed Speech Facilitates Word Segmentation," *Infancy* 7, no. 1 (2005): 53–71, https://doi.org/10.1207/s15327078in0701_5; Nairán Ramírez-Esparza, Adrián García-Sierra, and Patricia K. Kuhl, "Look Who's Talking: Speech Style and Social Context in Language Input to Infants Are Linked to Concurrent and Future Speech Development," *Developmental Science* 17, no. 6 (2014): 880–91, https://doi.org/10.1111/desc.12172.

83 **evokes a response from babies:** Roberta Michnick Golinkoff et al., "(Baby)Talk to Me: The Social Context of Infant-Directed Speech and Its Effects on Early Language Acquisition," *Current Directions in Psychological Science* 24, no. 5 (2015): 339–343, https://doi.org/10.1177/0963721415595345.

83 **greater influence on kids' vocabulary growth:** Meredith L. Rowe, "A Longitudinal Investigation of the Role of Quantity and Quality of Child-

Directed Speech in Vocabulary Development," *Child Development* 83, no. 5 (2012): 1762–74, https://doi.org/10.1111/j.1467-8624.2012.01805.x.

83 **positively related to kids' vocabulary skills a year later:** Rowe, "A Longitudinal Investigation."

84 **Numerous studies across the human lifespan:** Nicholas J. Cepeda et al., "Distributed Practice in Verbal Recall Tasks: A Review and Quantitative Synthesis," *Psychological Bulletin* 132, no. 3 (2006): 354–80, https://doi.org/10.1037/0033-2909.132.3.354.

84 **wide range of to-be-learned material:** Emilie Gerbier and Thomas C. Toppino, "The Effect of Distributed Practice: Neuroscience, Cognition, and Education," *Trends in Neuroscience and Education* 4, no. 3 (2015): 49–59, https://doi.org/10.1016/j.tine.2015.01.001.

84 **performed better:** Nancy J. Sullivan et al., "Simulation Exercise to Improve Retention of Cardiopulmonary Resuscitation Priorities for In-Hospital Cardiac Arrests: A Randomized Controlled Trial," *Resuscitation* 86 (January 1, 2015): 6–13, https://doi.org/10.1016/j.resuscitation.2014.10.021; Yiqun Lin et al., "Improving CPR Quality with Distributed Practice and Real-Time Feedback in Pediatric Healthcare Providers—A Randomized Controlled Trial," *Resuscitation* 130 (September 1, 2018): 6–12, https://doi.org/10.1016/j.resuscitation.2018.06.025.

84 **most replicated findings:** Haley A. Vlach, Catherine A. Bredemann, and Carla Kraft, "To Mass or Space? Young Children Do Not Possess Adults' Incorrect Biases About Spaced Learning," *Journal of Experimental Child Psychology* 183 (July 2019): 115–33, https://doi.org/10.1016/j.jecp.2019.02.003.

84 **a bias for massed learning:** Vlach, Bredemann, and Kraft, "To Mass or Space?"

86 **levels of personal relevance:** Stacy J. Priniski, Cameron A. Hecht, and Judith M. Harackiewicz, "Making Learning Personally Meaningful: A New Framework for Relevance Research," *The Journal of Experimental Education* 86, no. 1 (2018): 11–29, https://doi.org/10.1080/00220973.2017.1380589.

87 **your demeanor, engagement, and responsiveness:** Susan Sonnenschein and Kimberly Munsterman, "The Influence of Home-Based Reading Interactions on 5-Year-Olds' Reading Motivations and Early Literacy Development," *Early Childhood Research Quarterly* 17, no. 3 (2002): 318–37, https://doi.org/10.1016/S0885-2006(02)00167-9.

88 **Research by psychologist Carol Dweck and others:** Elizabeth A. Gunderson et al., "Parent Praise to Toddlers Predicts Fourth Grade Academic Achievement via Children's Incremental Mindsets," *Developmental Psychology* 54, no. 3 (2018): 397–409, https://doi.org/10.1037/dev0000444.

88 **a longitudinal study:** Gunderson et al., "Parent Praise."

5: NOURISHING WORDS: THE LASTING IMPACT OF EARLY LANGUAGE

93 **an unusual report:** Elizabeth Schaughency et al., "Developing a Community-Based Oral Language Preventive Intervention: Exploring Feasibility and Social Validity for Families Affected by the Canterbury Earthquakes," *Infants*

and Young Children 33, no. 3 (2020): 195–215, https://doi.org/10.1097 /IYC.0000000000000171.

93 **Building facades collapsed:** David Alexander, "Earthquake Rattles Christchurch, New Zealand," *New York Times*, September 3, 2010, https://www .nytimes.com/slideshow/2010/09/03/world/asia/new-zealand-earthquake.html.

93 **killed 185 people:** Charlotte Graham-McLay, "10 Years after Christchurch Quake, a Hush Where 8,000 Homes Once Stood," *New York Times*, February 21, 2021, https://www.nytimes.com/2021/02/21/world/australia/christchurch -new-zealand-quake-red-zone.html.

94 **performed worse on letter-word identification:** Celia J. Gomez and Hirokazu Yoshikawa, "Earthquake Effects: Estimating the Relationship Between Exposure to the 2010 Chilean Earthquake and Preschool Children's Early Cognitive and Executive Function Skills," *Early Childhood Research Quarterly* 38 (1st Quarter 2017): 127–36, https://doi.org/10.1016/j.ecresq.2016.08.004.

94 **struggled with expressive language:** Gail Gillon et al., "A Better Start to Literacy Learning: Findings from a Teacher-Implemented Intervention in Children's First Year at School," *Reading and Writing* 32, no. 8 (2019): 1994–95, https://doi.org/10.1007/s11145-018-9933-7.

94 **"potential developmental sequelae for children":** Schaughency et al., "Developing a Community-Based Oral Language Preventive Intervention," 196.

95 **many well-educated and advantaged families struggle with talk too:** Meredith L. Rowe, "Understanding Socioeconomic Differences in Parents' Speech to Children," *Child Development Perspectives* 12, no. 2 (2018): 122–25, https://doi.org/10.1111/cdep.12271.

95 **differences in healthcare outcomes:** Roberta Michnick Golinkoff et al., "Language Matters: Denying the Existence of the 30-Million-Word Gap Has Serious Consequences," *Child Development* 90, no. 3 (2019): 985–90, https:// doi.org/10.1111/cdev.13128.

95 **"Language is causally implicated":** Golinkoff et al., "Language Matters," 986.

96 **"no matter how accurately":** Anne E. Cunningham and Jamie Zibulsky, *Book Smart: How to Develop and Support Successful, Motivated Readers* (Oxford University Press, 2014), 14–15.

97 **"the single strongest action you can take to increase your child's educational opportunities":** Lauren Head Zauche et al., "The Power of Language Nutrition for Children's Brain Development, Health, and Future Academic Achievement," *Journal of Pediatric Health Care* 31, no. 4 (2017): 500, https://doi.org/10.1016/j .pedhc.2017.01.007.

97 **35 weeks gestation:** B. S. Kisilevsky et al., "Fetal Sensitivity to Properties of Maternal Speech and Language," *Infant Behavior and Development* 32, no. 1 (January 2009): 59–68, https://doi.org/10.1016/j.infbeh.2008.10.002; Jack P. Shonkoff and Deborah A. Phillips, eds., *From Neurons to Neighborhoods: The Science of Early Childhood Development* (National Academies Press, 2000), 187–90, https://doi.org/10.17226/9824.

97 **early-language environment predicts:** David K. Dickinson and Michelle V. Porche, "Relation Between Language Experiences in Preschool Classrooms and

Children's Kindergarten and Fourth-Grade Language and Reading Abilities," *Child Development* 82, no. 3 (2011): 872–81, https://doi.org/10.1111/j .1467-8624.2011.01576.x.

98 **statewide campaign called Talk With Me Baby:** Susan Brasher et al., "Integrating Early Brain Science and Skills into Prelicensure Nursing Curriculum to Promote Parent-Child Interaction," *Nurse Educator* 46, no. 4 (2021): E75—E77, https://doi.org/10.1097/NNE.0000000000000983.

98 **They use the *I Do*:** Douglas Fisher and Nancy Frey, "Gradual Release of Responsibility Instructional Framework," *IRA E-Ssentials*, October 18, 2013, 1–8, https://doi.org/10.1598/e-ssentials.8037.

98 **In the *I Do* step:** "NURSES," Talk With Me Baby, https://www.talkwithmebaby .org/nurses.

99 **Brains differ at birth:** Usha C. Goswami, *Child Psychology: A Very Short Introduction* (Oxford University Press, 2014), 6; Hakon Jonsson et al., "Differences Between Germline Genomes of Monozygotic Twins," *Nature Genetics* 53, no. 1 (2021): 27–33, https://doi.org/10.1038/s41588-020-00755-1.

99 **it's their environment that makes these differences trivial or meaningful:** Goswami, *Child Psychology*, 6.

100 **Child-directed speech supports language learning:** Golinkoff et al., "Language Matters," 987–88.

100 **infants prefer listening to this "baby talk":** Jessica F. Schwab and Casey Lew-Williams, "Language Learning, Socioeconomic Status, and Child-Directed Speech," *WIREs Cognitive Science* 7, no. 4 (2016): 265–69, https://doi .org/10.1002/wcs.1393.

101 **they match what they observe:** Margaret Addabbo et al., "'Something in the Way You Move': Infants Are Sensitive to Emotions Conveyed in Action Kinematics," *Developmental Science* 23, no. 1 (2020): e12873, https://doi.org/10 .1111/desc.12873.

101 **give your child the richest vocabulary, most fluent speech, and deepest background knowledge:** Ellen Bialystok, "Second-Language Acquisition and Bilingualism at an Early Age and the Impact on Early Cognitive Development," in R. E. Tremblay, R. G. Barr, and R. D. Peters, eds., *Encyclopedia on Early Childhood Development* (Centre of Excellence for Early Childhood Development, updated September 2017), 1–5, https://www.child-encyclopedia .com/pdf/expert/second-language/according-experts/second-language -acquisition-and-bilingualism-early-age-and-impact.

102 **help toddlers grasp common nouns:** Thea Cameron-Faulkner, Elena Lieven, and Michael Tomasello, "A Construction Based Analysis of Child Directed Speech," *Cognitive Science* 27, no. 6 (2003): 848–70, https://doi.org/10.1016/j .cogsci.2003.06.001.

102 **body movements capture infant attention:** Catherine S. Tamis-LeMonda, Yana Kuchirko, and Lulu Song, "Why Is Infant Language Learning Facilitated by Parental Responsiveness?," *Current Directions in Psychological Science* 23, no. 2 (2014): 123–24, https://doi.org/10.1177/0963721414522813.

102 **predictive of kids' language achievements:** Pamela Nicely, Catherine S. Tamis-

LeMonda, and Marc H. Bornstein, "Mothers' Attuned Responses to Infant Affect Expressivity Promote Earlier Achievement of Language Milestones," *Infant Behavior and Development* 22, no. 4 (1999): 557–66, https://doi.org /10.1016/S0163-6383(00)00023-0.

102 **There's evidence that by 11 months:** Ed Donnellan et al., "Infants' Intentionally Communicative Vocalizations Elicit Responses from Caregivers and Are the Best Predictors of the Transition to Language: A Longitudinal Investigation of Infants' Vocalizations, Gestures and Word Production," *Developmental Science* 23, no. 1 (2020): e12843, https://doi.org/10.1111 /desc.12843.

103 **1.4 million more words:** Jessica Logan et al., "When Children Are Not Read to at Home: The Million Word Gap," *Journal of Developmental and Behavioral Pediatrics* 40, no. 5 (2019): 384–85, https://doi.org/10.1097/DBP .0000000000000657.

103 **more varied, challenging, and enriching:** Dominic W. Massaro, "Two Different Communication Genres and Implications for Vocabulary Development and Learning to Read," *Journal of Literacy Research* 47, no. 4 (2015): 507–21, https://doi.org/10.1177/1086296X15627528.

103 **a style of reading aloud that fosters comment and discussion:** Schaughency et al., "Developing a Community-Based Oral Language Preventive Intervention," 195–218.

105 **"Part of mindfulness is":** *Ten Percent Happier Meditation*, iPhone app, v. 6.4.0 (10% Happier Inc., 2021); Joseph Goldstein, Essential Advice course, "Session 14: More Than a Hobby."

105 **Tuning in to your baby:** Carolyn Brockmeyer Cates et al., "Leveraging Healthcare to Promote Responsive Parenting: Impacts of the Video Interaction Project on Parenting Stress," *Journal of Child and Family Studies* 25, no. 3 (March 2016): 827–34, https://doi.org/10.1007/s10826-015-0267-7.

106 **coping mechanisms:** Cates et al., "Leveraging Healthcare," 829–33; Per Ivar Kaaresen et al., "A Randomized, Controlled Trial of the Effectiveness of an Early-Intervention Program in Reducing Parenting Stress after Preterm Birth," *Pediatrics* 118, no. 1 (2006): e10–e16, https://doi.org/10.1542/peds.2005-1491; Deborah Gross, Louis Fogg, and Sharon Tucker, "The Efficacy of Parent Training for Promoting Positive Parent–Toddler Relationships," *Research in Nursing and Health* 18, no. 6 (1995): 490–98, https://doi.org/10.1002 /nur.4770180605; Sharon Telleen, Allen Herzog, and Teresa Kilbane, "Impact of a Family Support Program on Mothers' Social Support and Parenting Stress," *American Journal of Orthopsychiatry* 59, no. 3 (1989): 410–18, https://doi.org /10.1111/j.1939-0025.1989.tb01676.x.

106 **a steep incline:** Keith A. Crnic and Cathryn L. Booth, "Mothers' and Fathers' Perceptions of Daily Hassles of Parenting Across Early Childhood," *Journal of Marriage and Family* 53, no. 4 (1991): 1043–45, https://doi.org/10.2307/353007; Marion O'Brien, "Child-Rearing Difficulties Reported by Parents of Infants and Toddlers," *Journal of Pediatric Psychology* 21, no. 3 (June 1996): 435–41, https:// doi.org/10.1093/jpepsy/21.3.433.

107 **Routine parenting work:** John Taylor, "Structural Validity of the Parenting Daily Hassles Intensity Scale," *Stress and Health* 35, no. 2 (2019): 176–85, https://doi.org/10.1002/smi.2852.

6: TAKING TURNS: HOW TO MAKE CONVERSATION A HABIT FROM DAY ONE

112 **enormous differences:** Meredith L. Rowe, "Understanding Socioeconomic Differences in Parents' Speech to Children," *Child Development Perspectives* 12, no. 2 (2018): 122–27, https://doi.org/10.1111/cdep.12271; Janellen Huttenlocher et al., "Sources of Variability in Children's Language Growth," *Cognitive Psychology* 61, no. 4 (2010): 343–65, https://doi.org/10.1016/j.cogpsych.2010 .08.002; Mary E. Brushe et al., "How Many Words Are Australian Children Hearing in the First Year of Life?," *BMC Pediatrics* 20, no. 52 (2020), 2–8, https://doi.org/10.1186/s12887-020-1946-0.

112 **Parent talkativeness varies:** Rowe, "Understanding Socioeconomic Differences," 123–24; Catherine S. Tamis-LeMonda, Yana Kuchirko, and Lulu Song, "Why Is Infant Language Learning Facilitated by Parental Responsiveness?," *Current Directions in Psychological Science* 23, no. 2 (2014): 121–26, https://doi.org/10 .1177/0963721414522813.

112 **talkative parents tend to have talkative little ones:** Jill Gilkerson and Jeffrey A. Richards, *The Power of Talk: Impact of Adult Talk, Conversational Turns, and TV During the Critical 0–4 Years of Child Development,* LENA Foundation Technical Report ITR-01-2 (LENA Foundation, 2009), 18.

112 **learning outcomes years later:** Lauren Head Zauche et al., "The Power of Language Nutrition for Children's Brain Development, Health, and Future Academic Achievement," *Journal of Pediatric Health Care* 31, no. 4 (2017): 493–503, https://doi.org/10.1016/j.pedhc.2017.01.007; David K. Dickinson and Michelle V. Porche, "Relation Between Language Experiences in Preschool Classrooms and Children's Kindergarten and Fourth-Grade Language and Reading Abilities," *Child Development* 82, no. 3 (2011): 870–86, https://doi.org /10.1111/j.1467-8624.2011.01576.x.

113 **overestimate how much they talk:** Jeffrey A. Richards et al., "How Much Do Parents Think They Talk to Their Child?," *Journal of Early Intervention* 39, no. 3 (2017): 163–79, https://doi.org/10.1177/1053815117714567.

114 **more than ten thousand children:** Steven M. Hannon, "Making a Difference: We Reached Our Goal to Impact 10,000 Children in 2019!," LENA, December 10, 2019, https://www.lena.org/year-in-review-2019/.

114 **separate talk and babbles from crying:** LENA, "LENA Pro," https://shop.lena .org/pages/download-center; LENA, "Understanding LENA Technology," https://www.lena.org/technology/.

114 **transcribed and coded the data by hand:** Betty Hart and Todd R. Risley, *Meaningful Differences in the Everyday Experience of Young American Children* (P. H. Brookes, 1995), 21–48.

114 **at least forty conversational turns:** LENA, *Inside Early Talk* (LENA Foundation, March 2021), 3–4, https://info.lena.org/inside-early-talk.

114 **peaks and valleys of talk:** LENA, *Inside Early Talk*, 6–7.

115 **In one viral video:** Meghan Holohan, "Dad Chats with Infant Son About TV Finale in Adorable Video," Today.com, June 5, 2019, https://www.today.com /parents/dad-chats-infant-son-about-tv-finale-adorable-video-t155568.

117 **Fogg recommends identifying:** BJ Fogg, *Tiny Habits: The Small Changes That Change Everything*, First Mariner Books ed. (Houghton Mifflin Harcourt, 2020), 6.

122 **Like so many of us:** Richards et al., "How Much Do Parents Think They Talk to Their Child?"

123 **1,139 adult words, 843 child vocalizations, and 194 conversational turns:** Mary E. Brushe et al., "Screen Time and Parent-Child Talk When Children Are Aged 12 to 36 Months," *JAMA Pediatrics* 178, no. 4 (2024): 369–75, https://doi .org/10.1001/jamapediatrics.2023.6790.

123 **toddlers struggle to learn from video:** Gabrielle A. Strouse et al., "Co-Viewing Supports Toddlers' Word Learning from Contingent and Noncontingent Video," *Journal of Experimental Child Psychology* 166 (February 1, 2018): 310–26, https://doi.org/10.1016/j.jecp.2017.09.005.

124 **"co-view, talk, and teach":** "Beyond Screen Time: Help Your Kids Build Healthy Media Use Habits," HealthyChildren.org, updated July 20, 2022, https://www.healthychildren.org/English/family-life/Media/Pages/Healthy -Digital-Media-Use-Habits-for-Babies-Toddlers-Preschoolers.aspx.

124 **negative correlation between hours of television:** Gilkerson and Richards, *The Power of Talk*, 16.

124 **worse performance on developmental screenings:** Sheri Madigan et al., "Association Between Screen Time and Children's Performance on a Developmental Screening Test," *JAMA Pediatrics* 173, no. 3 (2019): 244–50, https://doi.org/10.1001/jamapediatrics.2018.5056.

124 **valuable alphabetic knowledge:** Shalom M. Fisch, Rosemarie T. Truglio, and Charlotte F. Cole, "The Impact of *Sesame Street* on Preschool Children: A Review and Synthesis of 30 Years' Research," *Media Psychology* 1, no. 2 (1999): 165–90, https://doi.org/10.1207/s1532785xmep0102_5; Deborah L. Linebarger, "Super Why! to the Rescue: Can Preschoolers Learn Early Literacy Skills from Educational Television?," *International Journal for Cross-Disciplinary Subjects in Education* 6, no. 1 (2015): 2060–65, https://doi.org/10.20533/ijcdse.2042.6364 .2015.0286.

125 **"increase the burden for parents in later life":** Jin Zhao et al., "Excessive Screen Time and Psychosocial Well-Being: The Mediating Role of Body Mass Index, Sleep Duration, and Parent-Child Interaction," *The Journal of Pediatrics* 202 (November 2018): 161, https://doi.org/10.1016/j.jpeds.2018.06.029.

125 **screen-time exposure is associated with kids' increased risk:** Zhao et al., "Excessive Screen Time," 157–160.

125 **Thousands of families have signed on:** "Screen-Free Saturdays," Fairplay, https://www.screenfree.org/saturdays/.

126 **less engaged with and responsive to kids:** Brooke Auxier et al., *Parenting Children in the Age of Screens* (Pew Research Center, July 2020), 11–12, 47–49, 53–55, https://www.pewresearch.org/internet/wp-content/uploads /sites/9/2020/07/PI_2020.07.28_kids-and-screens_FINAL.pdf; Jenny Radesky

et al., "Maternal Mobile Device Use During a Structured Parent–Child Interaction Task," *Academic Pediatrics* 15, no. 2 (2015): 238–44, https://doi .org/10.1016/j.acap.2014.10.001; Cory A. Kildare and Wendy Middlemiss, "Impact of Parents Mobile Device Use on Parent-Child Interaction: A Literature Review," *Computers in Human Behavior* 75 (2017): 579–93, https://doi .org/10.1016/j.chb.2017.06.003.

126 **a survey of 2,000 parents:** "When It Comes to Screen Time, Parents Are Just as Guilty as Their Children," PR Newswire, October 21, 2019, https://www .prnewswire.com/news-releases/when-it-comes-to-screen-time-parents-are -just-as-guilty-as-their-children-300941553.html.

126 **"paying attention in a particular way":** Jon Kabat-Zinn, *Wherever You Go, There You Are: Mindfulness Meditation in Everyday Life,* 30th anniversary ed., rev. ed. (Hachette Go, 2023), 4.

127 **reduce caregiver stress and coparenting disagreements:** Virginia Burgdorf, Marianna Szabó, and Maree J. Abbott, "The Effect of Mindfulness Interventions for Parents on Parenting Stress and Youth Psychological Outcomes: A Systematic Review and Meta-Analysis," *Frontiers in Psychology* 10, no. 1336 (2019): 3–19, https://doi.org/10.3389/fpsyg.2019.01336; Susan M. Bögels, Annukka Lehtonen, and Kathleen Restifo, "Mindful Parenting in Mental Health Care," *Mindfulness* 1 (May 2010): 107–20, https://doi .org/10.1007/s12671-010-0014-5.

127 **reduction in the students' cravings for their smartphones:** Yukun Lan et al., "A Pilot Study of a Group Mindfulness-Based Cognitive-Behavioral Intervention for Smartphone Addiction Among University Students," *Journal of Behavioral Addictions* 7, no. 4 (2018): 1171–76, https://doi.org/10.1556/2006 .7.2018.103.

127 **"created room for more conscious decision-making":** Marta Brzosko, "How to Overcome Your Phone Addiction with Mindfulness," Better Humans, January 28, 2020, https://betterhumans.pub/how-to-overcome-your-phone-addiction -with-mindfulness-a48e2eae72ef.

127 **sit with our devices in hand:** Mitch Abblett, "Addicted to Your Phone? Try This Practice—Phone in Hand," *Mindful* (blog), March 14, 2016, https://www .mindful.org/addicted-to-your-phone-try-this-practice-phone-in-hand/.

127 **"We simply (and yet with great difficulty)":** Abblett, "Addicted to Your Phone?"

129 **recommends celebrating your habit three times:** Fogg, *Tiny Habits,* 151–52.

129 **"Emotions create habits":** Fogg, *Tiny Habits,* 137.

130 **predicted language skills eight months later:** Amber Muhinyi and Meredith L. Rowe, "Shared Reading with Preverbal Infants and Later Language Development," *Journal of Applied Developmental Psychology* 64 (July 1, 2019): 101053, https://doi.org/10.1016/j.appdev.2019.101053.

7: SOUND INSTRUCTION: THE TENOR OF READING SUCCESS

133 **Archival footage:** "Shirley Ellis 'The Name Game' (Merv Griffin Show 1965)," Dailymotion video, 5:04, https://www.dailymotion.com/video/x2xxzqn; "'The Name Game' by Shirley Ellis," YouTube video, 3:03, https://www.youtube.com /watch?v=LulWZQo46Ao.

133 **music history footnote:** "Hot Rhythm and Blues Singles," *Billboard (Archive: 1963–2000)* 77, no. 5 (1965): 14, Entertainment Industry Magazine Archive; Malcolm Baumgart and Mick Patrick, "The Name of the Game: The Story of Shirley Ellis," Spectropop, http://www.spectropop.com/ShirleyEllis/.

134 **Runway models walked:** Barry Janoff, "When Shopping at Kmart Can Be a 'Hazzard,'" *Brandweek*, May 8, 2006, 44; "Defining Moments," *WWD: Women's Wear Daily* 19, no. 69 (2006) 36–42.

134 **his "schtick with kids":** "'The Name Game' Is Howard's Secret Weapon with Children," Howard Stern, May 3, 2017, https://www.howardstern.com /show/2017/05/03/name-game-howards-secret-weapon-children/.

134 **trade articles:** Mark Holgate, "The Name Game," *Vogue,* July 2011, 68; Bernie Pacyniak, "The Name Game," *Candy Industry,* February 2004, 8.

134 **encyclopedia entry documenting *proto-rap*:** Eddie Bonilla, "Proto-Rap," in *St. James Encyclopedia of Hip Hop Culture*, ed. Thomas J. Riggs (St. James Press, 2018).

134 **nitty-gritty:** "The Nitty Gritty" was Ellis's first big hit, released by Congress Recordings in 1963. Phil Hardy, "Shirley Ellis," in *The Faber Companion to 20th Century Popular Music* (London: Faber and Faber, 2001).

136 **develops in a predictable sequence:** Jason L. Anthony and David J. Francis, "Development of Phonological Awareness," *Current Directions in Psychological Science* 14, no. 5 (2005): 255–59, https://doi.org/10.1111/j.0963-7214.2005 .00376.x.

136 **different presentations of the same fundamental ability:** Anthony and Francis, "Development of Phonological Awareness."

142 **transfers to phonological awareness and improves word-reading skills in English:** Jason L. Anthony et al., "Development of Bilingual Phonological Awareness in Spanish-Speaking English Language Learners: The Roles of Vocabulary, Letter Knowledge, and Prior Phonological Awareness," *Scientific Studies of Reading* 13, no. 6 (2009): 535–64, https://doi.org/10.1080/10888430 903034770; Aydin Y. Durgunoğlu, William E. Nagy, and Barbara J. Hancin-Bhatt, "Cross-Language Transfer of Phonological Awareness," *Journal of Educational Psychology* 85, no. 3 (1993): 453–65, https://doi.org/10.1037/0022 -0663.85.3.453.

143 **cross-language transfer:** Brenda A. Wawire and Young-Suk G. Kim, "Cross-Language Transfer of Phonological Awareness and Letter Knowledge: Causal Evidence and Nature of Transfer," *Scientific Studies of Reading* 22, no. 6 (2018): 443–61, https://doi.org/10.1080/10888438.2018.1474882; Hedi Kwakkel et al., "The Impact of Lexical Skills and Executive Functioning on L1 and L2 Phonological Awareness in Bilingual Kindergarten," *Learning and Individual Differences* 88 (May 1, 2021): 102009, https://doi.org/10.1016/j .lindif.2021.102009; Anthony et al., "Development of Bilingual Phonological Awareness"; Durgunoğlu et al., "Cross-Language Transfer."

143 **heavily influenced by oral-language ability:** Elinor Saiegh-Haddad, "What Is Phonological Awareness in L2?," *Journal of Neurolinguistics* 50 (May 1, 2019): 17–27, https://doi.org/10.1016/j.jneuroling.2017.11.001.

144 **"How can I teach reading":** Marcelle M. Haddix, *Cultivating Racial and*

Linguistic Diversity in Literacy Teacher Education: Teachers Like Me (Routledge, 2016), https://doi.org/10.4324/9781315850665.

145 **is spoken by the majority of black elementary schoolers in the United States:** Barbara Zurer Pearson, Tracy Conner, and Janiçe E. Jackson, "Removing Obstacles for African American English-Speaking Children Through Greater Understanding of Language Difference," *Developmental Psychology*, 49, no. 1 (2013): 31–44, https://doi.org/10.1037/a0028248.

146 **spell *ticket* as *tickit* at higher rates:** Rebecca Treiman and Margo Bowman, "Spelling in African American Children: The Case of Final Consonant Devoicing," *Reading and Writing* 28 (March 2015): 1013–28, https://doi.org/10.1007/s11145-015-9559-y.

146 **a handbook of linguistics:** Michael Hammond, "Prosodic Phonology," in *The Handbook of English Linguistics*, eds. Bas Aarts and April McMahon (Blackwell, 2006), 421–22.

8: L IS FOR LIBERATION: HOW TO HELP KIDS CRACK THE ALPHABETIC CODE

150 **"should know nothing but to obey his master":** Frederick Douglass, *Narrative of the Life of Frederick Douglass* (Oxford University Press, 1999), 39, EBSCO Publishing eBook Collection.

150 **down to the first joint:** Janet Cornelius, "'We Slipped and Learned to Read': Slave Accounts of the Literacy Process, 1830–1865," *Phylon (1960—)* 44, no. 3 (1983): 174, https://doi.org/10.2307/274930.

150 **stiffer and stiffer anti-literacy statutes:** Heather Andrea Williams, *Self-Taught: African American Education in Slavery and Freedom* (University of North Carolina Press, 2005), 205, 207–8.

150 **"Reading indicated to the world":** Williams, *Self-Taught*, 7.

151 **"the pathway from slavery to freedom":** Douglass, *Narrative of the Life*, 39.

151 **He mastered the letters:** Douglass, *Narrative of the Life*, 43, 46–47; David W. Blight, *Frederick Douglass: Prophet of Freedom* (Simon & Schuster, 2018), 42.

151 **5 percent succeeded:** James D. Anderson, *The Education of Blacks in the South, 1860–1935* (University of North Carolina Press, 1988), 16.

151 **"language of instruction":** Laura S. Tortorelli, Ryan P. Bowles, and Lori E. Skibbe, "Easy as AcHGzrjq: The Quick Letter Name Knowledge Assessment," *Reading Teacher* 71, no. 2 (2017): 146, https://doi.org/10.1002/trtr.1608.

152 **substantially fewer letter names:** Ryan P. Bowles et al., "Item Response Analysis of Uppercase and Lowercase Letter Name Knowledge," *Journal of Psychoeducational Assessment* 32, no. 2 (2014): 148–49, https://doi.org/10.1177/0734282913490266; Tara M. Strang and Shayne B. Piasta, "Socioeconomic Differences in Code-Focused Emergent Literacy Skills," *Reading and Writing* 29, no. 7 (2016): 1348, 1353–54, https://doi.org/10.1007/s11145-016-9639-7.

152 **likely to hear dialogue:** Tortorelli, Bowles, and Skibbe, "Easy as AcHGzrjq," 146.

152 **Letter names give:** Marilyn Jager Adams, *Beginning to Read: Thinking and Learning about Print* (MIT Press, 1994), 351.

152 **a tool for grasping and remembering the sounds:** Rebecca Treiman et al., "The Foundations of Literacy: Learning the Sounds of Letters," *Child Development* 69, no. 6 (1998): 1526–39, https://doi.org/10.2307/1132130; Laura M. Justice et al., "An Investigation of Four Hypotheses Concerning the Order by Which 4-Year-Old Children Learn the Alphabet Letters," *Early Childhood Research Quarterly* 21, no. 3 (2006): 379–84, https://doi.org/10.1016/j.ecresq .2006.07.010; Mary Ann Evans et al., "Letter Names, Letter Sounds and Phonological Awareness: An Examination of Kindergarten Children Across Letters and of Letters Across Children," *Reading and Writing* 19 (2006): 963–84, https://doi.org/10.1007/s11145-006-9026-x.

153 **foretelling later reading achievement:** Donna M. Scanlon and Frank R. Vellutino, "Prerequisite Skills, Early Instruction, and Success in First-Grade Reading: Selected Results from a Longitudinal Study," *Mental Retardation and Developmental Disabilities Research Reviews* 2 (1996): 57–58, https://doi.org/10 .1002/(SICI)1098-2779(1996)2:1<54::AID-MRDD9>3.0.CO;2-X.

153 **Preschool, kindergarten, and early intervention program curricula:** Francis L. Huang, "Does Attending a State-Funded Preschool Program Improve Letter Name Knowledge?," *Early Childhood Research Quarterly* 38 (2017): 117, https:// doi.org/10.1016/j.ecresq.2016.08.002.

153 **significantly fewer letter names:** Strang and Piasta, "Socioeconomic Differences," 1348–55.

153 **large-scale pre-K evaluation:** Huang, "Does Attending a State-Funded Preschool Program Improve Letter Name Knowledge?," 124.

154 **likely to struggle:** Shayne B. Piasta, Yaacov Petscher, and Laura M. Justice, "How Many Letters Should Preschoolers in Public Programs Know? The Diagnostic Efficiency of Various Preschool Letter-Naming Benchmarks for Predicting First-Grade Literacy Achievement," *Journal of Educational Psychology* 104, no. 4 (2012): 950–51, https://doi.org/10.1037/a0027757.

154 **many states' standards:** "English Language Arts Standards >> Reading: Foundational Skills >> Kindergarten >> 1 >> d," Common Core State Standards Initiative, http:// www.thecorestandards.org/ELA-Literacy/RF/K/1/d.

155 **compared with their colleagues in 1998:** Daphna Bassok, Scott Latham, and Anna Rorem, "Is Kindergarten the New First Grade?," *AERA Open* 1, no. 4 (2016): 5–6, https://doi.org/10.1177/2332858415616358.

155 **"more pronounced":** Bassok, Latham, and Rorem, "Is Kindergarten the New First Grade?," 14.

156 **2D marks to be deciphered:** Sarah Robins et al., "Parent–Child Conversations About Letters and Pictures," *Reading and Writing* 25 (2012): 2040, https://doi .org/10.1007/s11145-011-9344-5.

157 **In questionnaires:** Felicity Martini and Monique Sénéchal, "Learning Literacy Skills at Home: Parent Teaching, Expectations, and Child Interest," *Canadian Journal of Behavioural Science* 44, no. 3 (2012): 214–17, https://doi.org/10.1037 /a0026758.

157 **high expectations:** Martini and Sénéchal, "Learning Literacy Skills at Home," 212–13, 215.

157 **pioneering researcher Marilyn Jager Adams:** Adams, *Beginning to Read*, 351.

158 **labeled buckets:** Adams, *Beginning to Read*, 351.

158 **letter-name knowledge:** Rebecca Treiman and Sloane Wolter, "Use of Letter Names Benefits Young Children's Spelling," *Psychological Science* 31, no. 1 (2019): 4–5, https://doi.org/10.1177/0956797619888837.

158 **accelerates letter-sound learning:** Shayne B. Piasta and Richard K. Wagner, "Learning Letter Names and Sounds: Effects of Instruction, Letter Type, and Phonological Processing Skill," *Journal of Experimental Child Psychology* 105 (2010): 339, https://doi.org/10.1016/j.jecp.2009.12.008.

159 **Analyses of parent-child conversations:** Rebecca Treiman et al., "Parents' Talk About Letters with Their Young Children," *Child Development* 86, no. 5 (2015): 1415–16, https://doi.org/10.1111/cdev.12385.

160 **breaks and junctures within them:** Anna C. Both-de Vries and Adriana G. Bus, "Visual Processing of Pictures and Letters in Alphabet Books and the Implications for Letter Learning," *Contemporary Educational Psychology* 39, no. 2 (2014): 160–62, https://doi.org/10.1016/j.cedpsych.2014.03.005.

161 **from A to Z:** Cindy D. Jones and D. Ray Reutzel, "Enhanced Alphabet Knowledge Instruction: Exploring a Change of Frequency, Focus, and Distributed Cycles of Review," *Reading Psychology* 33, no. 5 (2012): 449, https://doi.org/10.1080/02702711.2010.545260.

162 **are among the easiest to name and write:** Shayne B. Piasta, "Moving to Assessment-Guided Differentiated Instruction to Support Young Children's Alphabet Knowledge," *Reading Teacher* 68, no. 3 (2014): 206, https://doi.org/10.1002/trtr.1316; Beth M. Phillips et al., "IRTs of the ABCs: Children's Letter Name Acquisition," *Journal of School Psychology* 50, no. 4 (2012): 468–74, https://doi.org/10.1016/j.jsp.2012.05.002; Laura M. Justice et al., "An Investigation of Four Hypotheses Concerning the Order by Which 4-Year-Old Children Learn the Alphabet Letters," *Early Childhood Research Quarterly* 21 (2006), 381; Cynthia Puranik, Yaacov Petscher, and Christopher Lonigan, "Dimensionality and Reliability of Letter Writing in 3- to 5-Year-Old Preschool Children," *Learning and Individual Differences* 28 (2013): 138–39.

162 **stronger readers at the end of kindergarten:** Treiman et al., "Parents' Talk About Letters with Their Young Children," 1411–12.

162 **wide array of early-childhood programs:** Phillips et al., "IRTs of the ABCs."

162 **a "typical order":** Piasta, "Moving to Assessment-Guided Differentiated Instruction," 206.

163 **faster pace of letter instruction:** Kristin Sunde, Bjarte Furnes, and Kjersti Lundetræ, "Does Introducing the Letters Faster Boost the Development of Children's Letter Knowledge, Word Reading and Spelling in the First Year of School?," *Scientific Studies of Reading* 24, no. 2 (2020): 142–55, https://doi.org/10.1080/10888438.2019.1615491.

164 **Researchers estimate:** Both-de Vries and Bus, "Visual Processing of Pictures and Letters," 160.

165 **embedded in the signs and labels:** Michelle M. Neumann, "The Effects of a Parent–Child Environmental Print Program on Emergent Literacy," *Journal of Early Childhood Research* 16, no. 4 (2018): 338, https://doi.org/10.1177/1476718X18809120.

165 **use multisensory strategies:** Neumann, "The Effects of a Parent–Child Environmental Print Program," 339–43.

165 **Texas Book Festival:** Meg Medina, Ibtihaj Muhammad, and Ibi Zoboi, panelists, "When I Was a Kid: Writing Books Inspired by Our Childhoods," moderated by Mary Ann Fitch, Texas Book Festival, Austin, TX, October 26, 2019.

9. WORD WISDOM: HOW TO SPELL YOUR WAY TO BETTER READING

169 **first black student to make it to the final round:** Maria Cramer and Alexandra E. Petri, "Behind Zaila Avant-garde's Win, a History of Struggle for Black Spellers," *New York Times*, July 11, 2021, https://www.nytimes.com/2021/07/11/us/spelling-bee-racism-zaila-avant-garde.html.

170 **excavated Cox's incredible story:** Michael Romain, "The Tragedy of MacNolia Cox," May 20, 2015, *Wednesday Journal of Oak Park and River Forest*, May 20, 2015, https://www.oakpark.com/2015/05/20/the-tragedy-of-macnolia-cox/.

170 **ride in segregated train cars:** April White, "Spelling Bee Champ Zaila Avant-garde Was Inspired by a Black Girl Named MacNolia Cox. This Is Why," *The Washington Post*, July 10, 2021, https://www.washingtonpost.com/history/2021/07/10/macnolia-cox-zaila-avant-garde-spelling-bee/.

170 **Cox spelled flawlessly:** Romain, "The Tragedy of MacNolia Cox."

170 **a word that wasn't on the approved list:** Cramer and Petri, "Behind Zaila Avant-garde's Win."

170 **died of cancer, a domestic:** White, "Spelling Bee Champ"; Romain, "The Tragedy of MacNolia Cox."

170 **tells Cox's life story in reverse:** A. Van Jordan, *M-A-C-N-O-L-I-A: Poems* (W. W. Norton & Company, 2004).

170 **"Historically, African-Americans have understood":** Cynthia R. Greenlee, "The Word Is 'Nemesis': The Fight to Integrate the National Spelling Bee," *Longreads*, June 5, 2017, https://longreads.com/2017/06/05/the-word-is-nemesis-the-fight-to-integrate-the-national-spelling-bee/.

171 **Errors in job applications:** Christelle Martin-Lacroux and Alain Lacroux, "Do Employers Forgive Applicants' Bad Spelling in Résumés?," *Business and Professional Communication Quarterly*, 80, no. 3 (2017), 321–35, https://doi.org/10.1177/2329490616671310; Christelle Martin-Lacroux, "'Without the Spelling Errors I Would Have Shortlisted Her . . . ': The Impact of Spelling Errors on Recruiters' Choice During the Personnel Selection Process," *International Journal of Selection and Assessment* 25, no. 3 (2017): 276–83, https://doi.org/10.1111/ijsa.12179.

172 **the faster you'll read the word:** Sandra Martin-Chang, Gene Ouellette, and Melanie Madden, "Does Poor Spelling Equate to Slow Reading? The Relationship Between Reading, Spelling, and Orthographic Quality," *Reading and Writing* 27, no. 8 (2014): 1485–505, https://doi.org/10.1007/s11145-014-9502-7; Gene Ouellette, Sandra Martin-Chang, and Maya Rossi, "Learning from Our Mistakes: Improvements in Spelling Lead to Gains in Reading Speed," *Scientific Studies of Reading* 21, no. 4 (2017): 350–57, https://doi.org/10.1080/10888438.2017.1306064; Maya Rossi, Sandra Martin-Chang, and Gene Ouellette, "Exploring the Space Between Good and Poor Spelling:

Orthographic Quality and Reading Speed," *Scientific Studies of Reading* 23, no. 2 (2019): 192–201, https://doi.org/10.1080/10888438.2018.1508213.

172 **directly linked to reading fluency and even third-grade reading:** David D. Paige et al., "A Path Analytic Model Linking Foundational Skills to Grade 3 State Reading Achievement," *Journal of Educational Research* (2018): 110–20, https://doi.org/10.1080/00220671.2018.1445609.

172 **supporting better phonological awareness and reading skills:** Steve Graham and Tanya Santangelo, "Does Spelling Instruction Make Students Better Spellers, Readers, and Writers? A Meta-Analytic Review," *Reading and Writing* 27 (2014): 1703–43, https://doi.org/10.1007/s11145-014-9517-0; R. Malatesha Joshi et al., "How Words Cast Their Spell," *American Educator* 32 (Winter 2008–2009): 6–43, https://www.aft.org/sites/default/files/joshi.pdf.

173 **at risk of receiving lower grades in other subjects:** Steve Graham, Karen R. Harris, and Michael Hebert, "It Is More Than Just the Message: Analysis of Presentation Effects in Scoring Writing," *Focus on Exceptional Children* 44, no. 4 (2011): 1–12.

173 **"the abandoned stepchild in the family of language arts":** Joshi et al., "How Words Cast Their Spell," 9.

173 **the vast majority of elementary school teachers say:** Antoinette Doyle, Jing Zhang, and Chris Mattatall, "Spelling Instruction in the Primary Grades: Teachers' Beliefs, Practices, and Concerns," *Reading Horizons* 54, no. 2 (2015): 21, https://scholarworks.wmich.edu/reading_horizons/vol54/iss2/2/; Francine R. Johnston, "Exploring Classroom Teachers' Spelling Practices and Beliefs," *Reading Research and Instruction* 40, no. 2 (2000): 143–55, 150, https://doi.org/10.1080/19388070109558339.

175 **tend to write common letters (e.g., E, T, and A) more:** Rebecca Treiman et al., "Statistical Learning and Spelling: Older Prephonological Spellers Produce More Wordlike Spellings Than Younger Prephonological Spellers," *Child Development* 89, no. 4 (2018): e431–e443; https://doi.org/10.1111/cdev.12893.

175 **Letters from their own names, and letter combinations:** Treiman et al., "Older Prephonological Spellers."

175 *statistical learning*: Treiman et al., "Older Prephonological Spellers," e431–e432; Rebecca Treiman, "Teaching and Learning Spelling," *Child Development Perspectives* 12, no. 4 (2018): 235–39, https://doi.org/10.1111/cdep.12292; Rebecca Treiman, "Statistical Learning and Spelling," *Language, Speech, and Hearing Services in Schools* 49, no. 3S (2018): 644–52, https://doi.org/10.1044/2018_LSHSS-STLT1-17-0122.

177 **"Allowing children to engage":** Gene Ouellette and Monique Sénéchal, "Invented Spelling in Kindergarten as a Predictor of Reading and Spelling in Grade 1: A New Pathway to Literacy, or Just the Same Road, Less Known?," *Developmental Psychology* 53, no. 1 (2017): 77–88, https://doi.org/10.1037/dev0000179.

184 **a nearly universal method:** Gary Libben, Christina L. Gagné, and Wolfgang U. Dressler, "The Representation and Processing of Compound Words," in *Word Knowledge and Word Usage: A Cross-Disciplinary Guide to the Mental Lexicon*,

vol. 337, eds. Vito Pirrelli, Ingo Plag, and Wolfgang U. Dressler (De Gruyter Mouton, 2020), 336–42, https://doi.org/10.1515/9783110440577.

185 **present with various spellings since Middle English:** Barry J. Blake, "Sound Symbolism in English: Weighing the Evidence," *Australian Journal of Linguistics* 37, no. 3 (2017): 286–313, https://doi.org/10.1080/07268602.2017.1298394.

185 **Some physicians think it's time to abandon eponyms:** Alexander Woywodt and Eric Matteson, "Should Eponyms Be Abandoned? Yes," *BMJ* 335 (September 2007): 424, https://doi.org/10.1136/bmj.39308.342639.AD.

187 *portmanteaus,* **after stiff leather suitcases:** Lewis Carroll, *Alice's Adventures in Wonderland and Other Classic Works* (New York: Fall River Press, 2014), 198–99.

188 **partial list of the spelling knowledge and skills:** "English Language Arts Standards," Common Core State Standards Initiative, accessed January 11, 2022, https://www.thecorestandards.org/ELA-Literacy/; "Texas Administrative Code: Texas Essential Knowledge and Skills for English Language Arts and Reading: Elementary," Texas Education Agency, accessed January 11, 2022, https://texreg.sos.state.tx.us/public/readtac$ext.ViewTAC?tac_view=5&ti=19&pt=2&ch=110&sch=A&rl=Y; Joshi et al., "How Words Cast Their Spell"; Misty Adoniou, *Spelling It Out: How Words Work and How to Teach Them* (Port Melbourne, Victoria: Cambridge University Press, 2016), 130–31.

191 **devote considerable time:** Shalini Shankar, *Beeline: What Spelling Bees Reveal About Generation Z's New Path to Success* (Basic Books, 2019), chap. 5.

191 **Edith Fuller was just 5 years old:** Katie Kindelan, "6-Year-Old Is Youngest Competitor at the Scripps National Spelling Bee," ABC News, https://abcnews.go.com/Lifestyle/year-youngest-competitor-scripps-national-spelling-bee/story?id=47728060.

191 **hours preparing study materials:** Shankar, *Beeline*, chaps. 1, 2, 5.

192 **pronouncing *righteous* as "ri-tee-us":** Shankar, *Beeline*, 137–38.

192 **studied seven hours a day:** Janell Ross, "Zaila Avant-garde Knows the Troubling History Behind Her Historic Spelling Bee Win," *Time*, July 18, 2021, https://time.com/6080654/zaila-avant-garde-spelling-bee-equality/.

192 **"astounding progress":** Shalini Shankar, "Shankar: Zaila Avant-garde—2021 Scripps National Spelling Bee Champ—Stands Where Black Children Were Once Kept Out," *The Palm Beach Post,* July 14, 2021, https://www.palmbeachpost.com/story/opinion/columns/2021/07/14/zaila-avant-garde-2021-scripps-national-spelling-bee-champ-stands-where-black-children-were-once-kep/7944678002/.

193 **spending her $10,000 prize winnings:** Ben Nuckols, "Louisiana Teen Is More Than a Spelling Bee Finalist. She's a 3x World Record Holder," NOLA.com, July 9, 2021, https://www.nola.com/news/louisiana-teen-is-more-than-a-spelling-bee-finalist-shes-a-3x-world-record-holder/article_febe1422-e02a-11eb-889f-67c4e39efe78.html.

10. PATHFINDING: HOW SAVVY PARENTS KEEP LEARNING AND LEADING

206 *four* **studies with different methods:** Lisa S. Scott and Alexandra Monesson, "The Origin of Biases in Face Perception," *Psychological Science* 20, no. 6 (2009):

676–80, https://doi.org/10.1111%2Fj.1467-9280.2009.02348.x; Lisa S. Scott and Alexandra Monesson, "Experience-Dependent Neural Specialization During Infancy," *Neuropsychologia* 48, no. 6 (2010): 1857–61, https://doi.org/10 .1016/j.neuropsychologia.2010.02.008; Lisa S. Scott, "Mechanisms Underlying the Emergence of Object Representations During Infancy," *Journal of Cognitive Neuroscience* 23, no. 10 (2011): 2935–44, https://doi.org/10.1162/jocn_a_00019; Charisse B. Pickron et al., "Learning to Individuate: The Specificity of Labels Differentially Impacts Infant Visual Attention," *Child Development* 89, no. 3 (May/June 2018): 698–710, https://doi.org/10.1111/cdev.13004.

206 **mini-sitcom public service announcement:** New America, "Read the Right Books at the Right Time: A Learning Sciences Exchange Fellows' Project," YouTube video, 8:37, https://www.youtube.com/watch?v=UtNANpAyQOw.

207 **picked up in media:** Lisa S. Scott, "Brain Study Suggests the Type of Book You Read to Your Baby Is Important," *The Washington Post*, December 31, 2017, https://www.washingtonpost.com/national/health-science/brain-study-suggests -the-type-of-book-you-read-to-your-baby-is-important/2017/12/29/c1cec97e -ea5d-11e7-9f92-10a2203f6c8d_story.html; Lisa Scott, "Lisa Scott: For Baby's Brain to Benefit, Read the Right Books at the Right Time," *New Zealand Herald*, December 10, 2017, https://www.nzherald.co.nz/lifestyle/lisa-scott-for -babys-brain-to-benefit-read-the-right-books-at-the-right-time/7LO2YRJJ25BB 6UHMMW2MNKBBCA/.

207 **"Each one answers the question":** Kim Tingley, "How Much Alcohol Can You Drink Safely?," *The New York Times Magazine*, May 16, 2019, https://www .nytimes.com/2019/05/16/magazine/how-much-alcohol-can-you-drink-safe -health.html.

CONCLUSION: RAISING ALL READERS

214 **Lucy Goode Brooks:** John T. Kneebone and the *Dictionary of Virginia Biography*, "Lucy Goode Brooks (1818–1900)," *Encyclopedia Virginia*, http://www .EncyclopediaVirginia.org/Brooks_Lucy_Goode_1818-1900.

Index

Note: Italicized page numbers indicate material in photographs or illustrations.